The Midlands

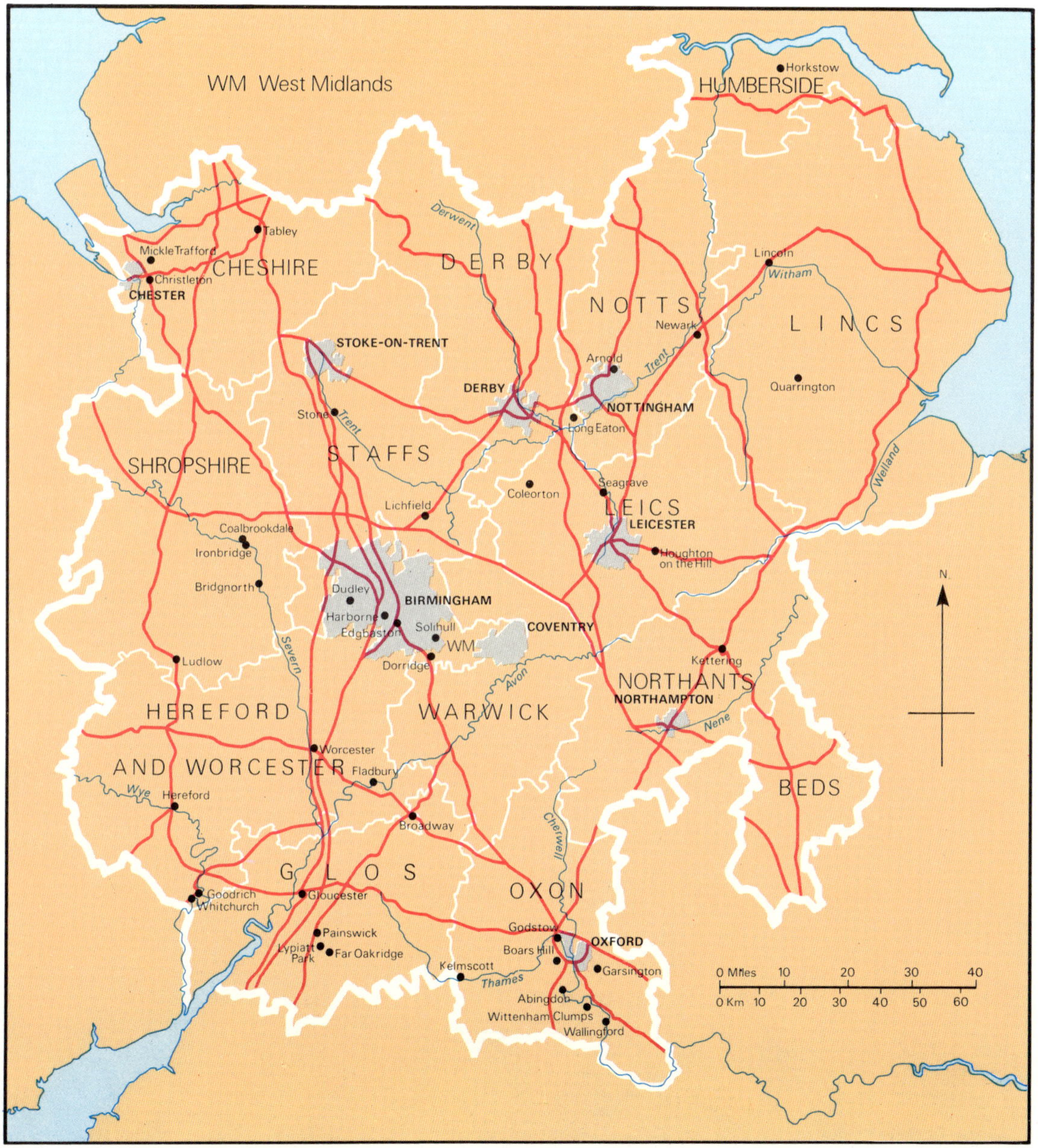

INTRODUCTION

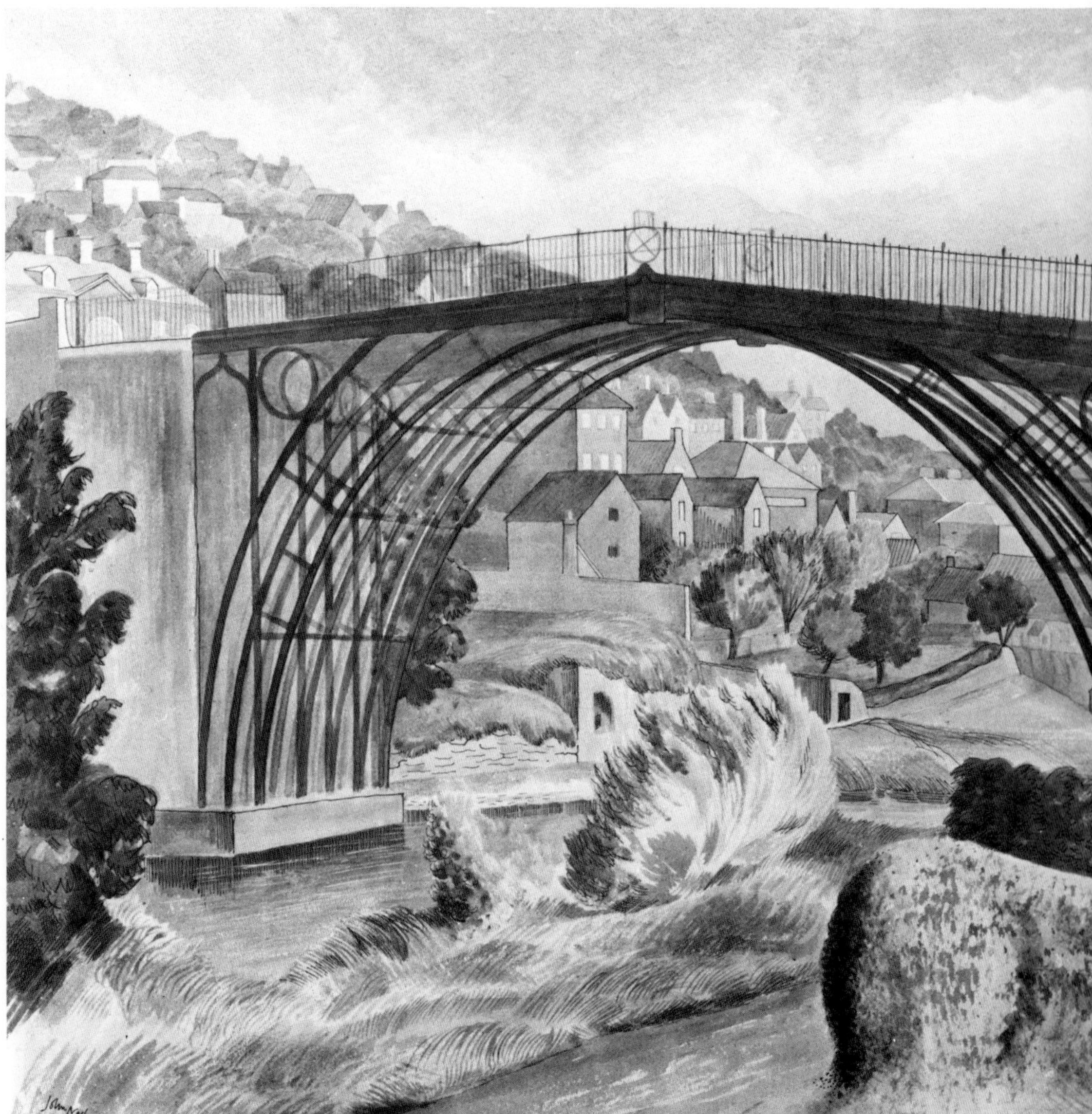

The area to the south of Birmingham is often referred to as 'Shakespeare Country' and, with its orchards and half-timbered cottages bordering on the River Avon, has come to embody for many the spirit of rural England. It was at Broadway – now one of the most self-consciously pretty villages in this part of the country – that the American artist John Singer Sargent painted vivid impressions of an idyllic English summer. Today one has to go further west, to the counties bordering on Wales, to find scenery that is genuinely unspoilt; but it was ironically here, at Ironbridge in Shropshire, that the Industrial Revolution had its origins in the late eighteenth century.

The relics of the country's industrial past have, in their abandoned and often overgrown state, succumbed to the beauty of their natural surroundings. One accords them now the stature generally reserved for classical ruins. Yet even in their own time, places like Ironbridge were considerable tourist attractions. To eighteenth-century taste there was as much to admire in the sight of smoke and flames emanating from furnaces as there was in that of Vesuvius erupting. This is exemplified in de Loutherbourg's famous *Coalbrookdale by Night*. Another painter who captured something of the wonder and awe inspired by the birth of the industrial age was Joseph Wright of Derby. Wright, one of the few famous artists to have spent a substantial part of his career in the Midlands, lent an air of mystery to the world of science and technology by investing it with a dramatic chiaroscuro derived from Caravaggio.

The reality of industrial England is a rather different and drearier matter. The Midlands have known no painter equal in stature to native writers such as Arnold Bennett and D. H. Lawrence, who have concerned themselves with the life and character of the urban environment. It is symptomatic that the only important group of painters to have worked in Birmingham was associated with the Tempera Revival, a nostalgic movement which looked back to the art and life of the fifteenth century. While they at least worked for a period in their native city, most of the artists born in the industrial towns of the Midlands have tended to forsake their home surroundings at a relatively early age, seldom to return.

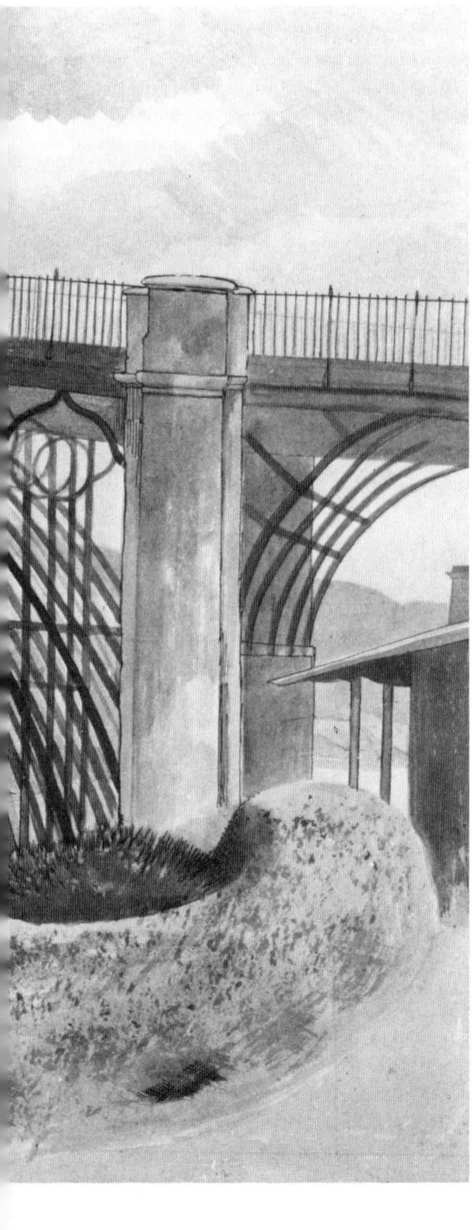

John Nash
Ironbridge
1952; watercolour, pen and ink and pencil, 40·6 × 61 cm
Ironbridge Gorge Museum

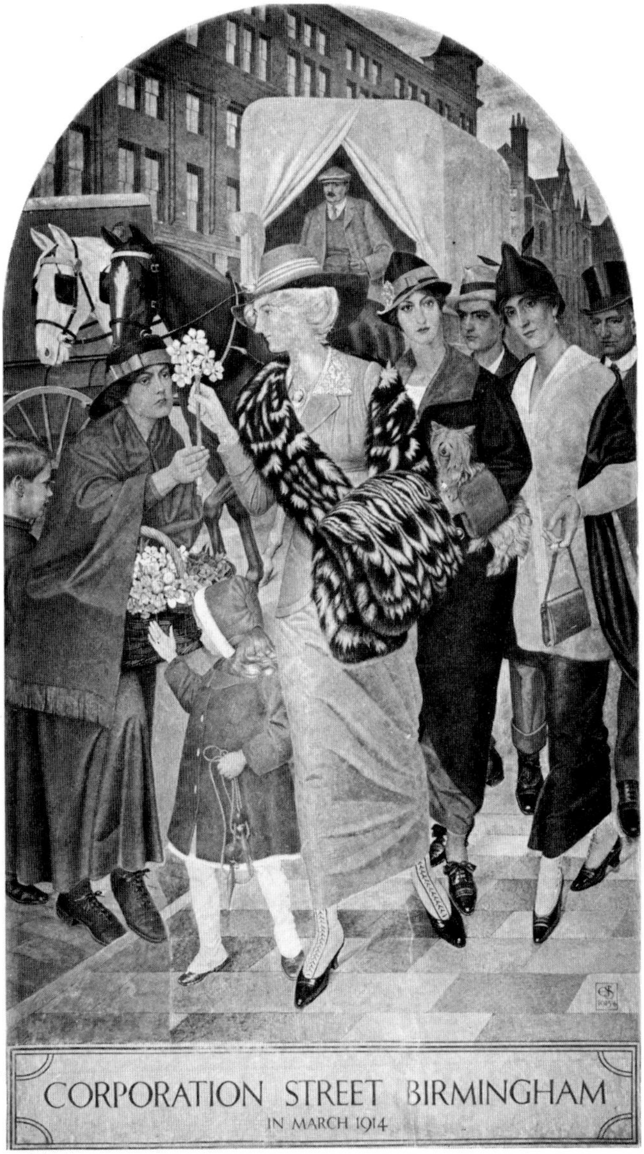

Joseph Edward Southall
Corporation Street, Birmingham, in March 1914
1915–16; fresco, 279·4 × 162·5 cm
Birmingham City Art Gallery

Birmingham, *West Midlands*

David Cox, the watercolour painter, was born in 1783 in a small house (now gone) on Heathmill Lane in the south-eastern part of Birmingham. He was a pupil of the local artist and drawing-master Joseph Barber, but spent most of his career in London and Hereford; he returned to the Birmingham area in later life, however, taking Greenfield House (plaque) in Greenfield Lane, Harborne. He lived here from 1841 until his death in 1859. A leading landscapist of the next generation who was also brought up in Birmingham was Thomas Creswick; he trained here under J. V. Barber, the son of Cox's master.

No. 11 Bennett's Hill (gone; the site is now a building society) was the childhood home of Edward Burne-Jones. He was born here in 1833, the son of a carver and gilder, and grew up in an environment that his wife later described as 'destitute of any visible thing that could appeal to the imagination'. While a pupil at King Edward's School (then in New Street, near his house), Burne-Jones was already developing an interest in medieval religion and would playfully sign letters 'Edward Cardinal de Byrmyngham'. His enthusiasm was deepened by life at Oxford, where he became an undergraduate in 1853.

Henry Tonks, the great Slade School teacher, was born in Solihull in 1862; his family moved soon afterwards to Packwood Grange in Dorridge (gone; the site is at the corner of Earlswood Road and Grange Road), where the artist spent his childhood.

A close contemporary of Tonks was Joseph Southall. His family were in Nottingham when he was born (in 1861), but they came to Birmingham in the following year and Southall remained here for the rest of his career, living for most of it at 13 Charlotte Road in Edgbaston. Deeply impressed by a visit to Italy in 1883, he abandoned his original intention of becoming an architect and turned to art. He spent the next eight years mastering the technique of tempera painting, 'this most beautiful and permanent method, in which most of the best Italian pictures were wrought up to the middle of the sixteenth century'. As a teacher at the Birmingham School of Art, Southall influenced many young artists and led a 'tempera revival' which flourished around the turn of the century and included Charles Gere and Arthur Gaskin among its most talented adherents. During the First World War he was commissioned to paint frescoes of Birmingham scenes in the City Art Gallery; in addition to these works, the gallery now contains a room devoted to pictures by Southall and other tempera revivalists.

Boars Hill, *Oxon.*

During the Second World War Paul Nash lived with friends in a house called Sandylands (now renamed Aldoth) in Hamel's Lane, Boars Hill. From the garden of the house the distinct outline of two domed or mammiform hills called Wittenham Clumps could be seen far in the distance. As a young man Nash had accompanied his parents when they stayed with relatives who lived close to the Clumps at Sinodun House

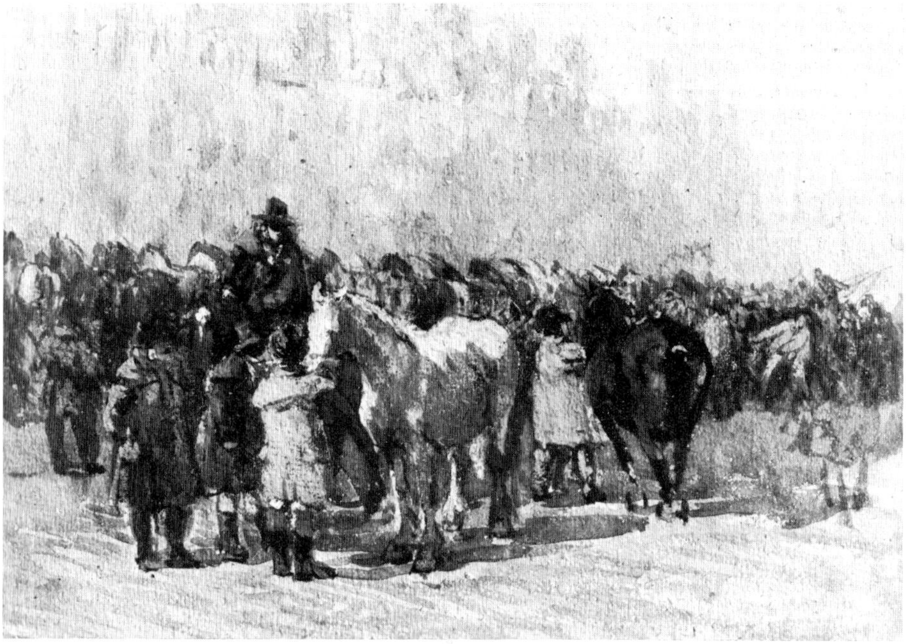

David Cox
The Birmingham Horse Fair
Watercolour, 18·4 × 26·3 cm
Birmingham City Art Gallery

Paul Nash
Landscape of the Vernal Equinox
1943–4; oil on canvas, 69·8 × 91·4 cm
Collection of H.M. The Queen Mother

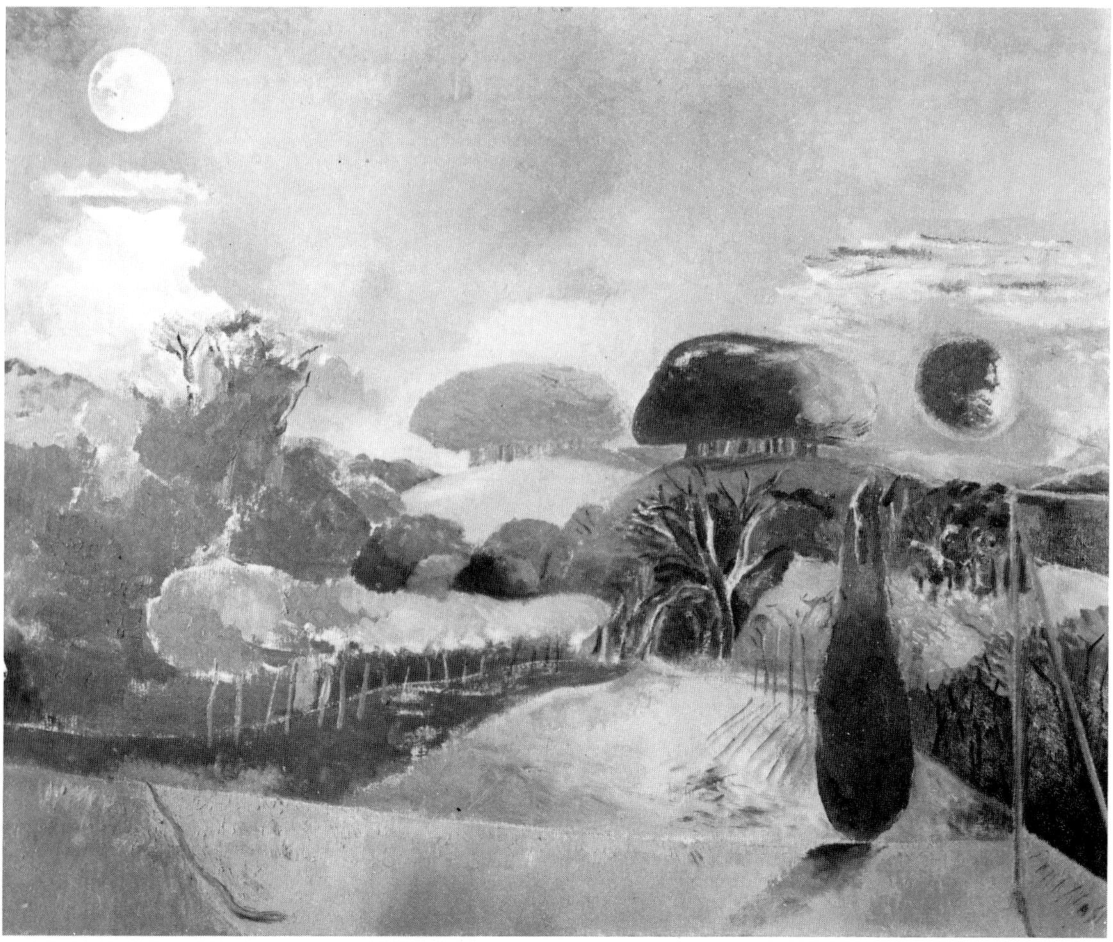

near Wallingford. He had always been intrigued by them, and described them in 1911 as 'grey hallowed hills crowned by old trees, Pan-ish places down by the river wonderful to think on, full of strange enchantment . . . a beautiful legendary country haunted by old Gods long forgotten'. Indeed, they were to be the most persistent motif of his art, appearing again and again throughout his career but given their fullest expression in the mystical landscapes painted at Sandylands. In his own words, these are virtually all 're-creations of one actual scene – the prospect or scene from the house I go to stay at in Boars Hill where there is a wide window . . . looking across the garden to the Berkshire Downs on the horizon. Between the farthest woods on the downs rise up the twin hills of the Wittenham Clumps. Actually they are a long way away from Boars Hill and I have to look at them through my field glasses to get an adequate view of them.' Today the view has been impaired by modern buildings.

Broadway, *Hereford and Worcester*

John Singer Sargent paid three visits to Worcestershire in the 1880s and executed here some of his finest English landscapes, as well as his best-known imaginative composition, *Carnation, Lily, Lily, Rose.* Born in Florence in 1856 of itinerant American parents, Sargent studied painting in Paris under Carolus-Duran; he intended to remain in Paris, but the scandal caused by his portrait of a Parisian beauty in daring *décolletage* made him decide to come to England. He paid a brief visit to this country in 1884 and moved here permanently in the following year. In the summer of 1885 he went on a boating trip on the Thames with an American painter, Edwin Austin Abbey, and, jumping into the water, cut his head open on a concealed spike. Abbey took him to convalesce at the Worcestershire village of Broadway, where at Farnham House an American illustrator called Frank Millet was staying, whom Sargent had known in Paris. Millet and his wife Lily had gathered round them at Broadway a group of American artists. The atmosphere of the house was exceptionally congenial, and Sargent soon found himself the centre of attention. For the first time since he had moved to England, his brilliant abilities as a painter were met with universal recognition. At Broadway Sargent was introduced to Henry James and Edmund Gosse, both of whom were frequent guests of the Millets. By coincidence the two writers had already written enthusiastically about Sargent, and had been among his first supporters; they now became his lifelong friends, as well as his most articulate spokesmen.

Life at Broadway was distinctly relaxing and entertaining: during the day the guests indulged in some not altogether serious painting or writing, then played tennis in the late afternoon and early evening, and finally, after dinner, took part in what Frank Millet described as 'various cheering games in the studio'. Edmund Gosse later remembered a small medieval ruin in the garden where 'Henry James and I would write, while Abbey and Millet painted on the floor below, and Sargent and Parsons tilted their easels just outside. We were all within shouting distance, and not much serious work was done, for we were in towering spirits and everything was food for laughter'.

Later at Broadway, Sargent began to take an interest in the effect of twilight on figures. At first he used as his model Millet's daughter Kate, whose black hair he covered with a blond wig. Towards the end of the summer, however, the French painter Fred Barnard arrived, and with him his two golden-haired daughters. The two girls had just the colour of hair required by Sargent for his studies, and Kate, much to her disappointment, was superseded as his model. Using the Barnard girls, Sargent evolved a most ambitious canvas, in which the twilight effect was heightened by illuminated paper lanterns. Every evening a strange ritual in preparation for this painting took place in the Farnham House garden: the girls would put on white dresses, the easel was meticulously positioned, and lilies which normally stood in pots on the ground were raised on chairs. Everyone, including Sargent, then resumed the daily game of tennis and continued until the light was judged by the artist to be suitable for his painting. Then, in Gosse's words, 'the game was stopped, and the painter was accompanied to the scene of his labours. Instantly he took up his place at a distance from the canvas, and at a certain notation of the light ran forward over the lawn with the action of a wag-tail, planting at the same time rapid dots of paint on the picture, and then retiring again, only with equal suddenness to repeat the wag-tail action. All this occupied but two or three minutes, the light rapidly declining, and then, while he left the young ladies to remove his machinery, Sargent would join us again, so long as the twilight permitted, in a last turn at lawn tennis.' Sargent obviously relished playing to an audience, but at heart he was not so confident about his talents, and once confessed to Gosse at Broadway that he was thinking of giving up painting altogether and becoming a musician or even a businessman.

Sargent continued his painting of Barnard's daughters late into the autumn. Eventually he returned to London, and the half-completed painting was stored in a barn at Farnham House. When he returned the following summer the Millets had moved to nearby Russell House, which had the advantage of a much larger garden. Sargent resumed work on his ambitious canvas, and decided on a background featuring a wealth of different flowers. He toured around the local countryside in search of roses, carnations and lilies, which he replanted in the Millets' garden. By the end of the autumn his work was completed, and he entitled it *Carnation, Lily, Lily, Rose* after a favourite song. The title might als be an unconscious reference to Lily Millet, to whom he was very attracted at the time. When exhibited at the Royal Academy in 1887, this vividly coloured painting was a sensation and earned the artist considerable fame.

It was as a very successful and established painter that Sargent returned to Worcestershire in the summer of 1889. This time he rented, with his parents and sister, the rectory at the village of Fladbury (near Pershore), about twelve miles from Broadway. Among the many guests who came to visit him here was another painter friend from Paris days, Paul Helleu. Helleu was on his honeymoon, and arrived with a beautiful sixteen-year-old girl. The couple would accompany Sargent when he took a boat across the River Avon to the edge of the water-meadows directly opposite the rectory. Once here, Sargent and Helleu would begin painting. Bored as Helleu's wife was by having to wait while her two companions were at work, her doe-like features and long red hair lent extra enchantment to the scene. Earlier in the summer Sargent had been to see Monet at Giverny and had profited enormously from the visit. The landscapes with figures that he subsequently painted at Fladbury must be counted among the most successful assimilations in England of the Impressionist idiom.

Chester, *Cheshire*

Chester was the birthplace of the popular Victorian illustrator Randolph Caldecott. He was the son of a merchant hatter and attended the King Henry VIII School. At fifteen, however, he left home to work as a bank-clerk, eventually moving to Manchester.

The year Caldecott left, 1861, saw the arrival of the Liverpool animal-painter

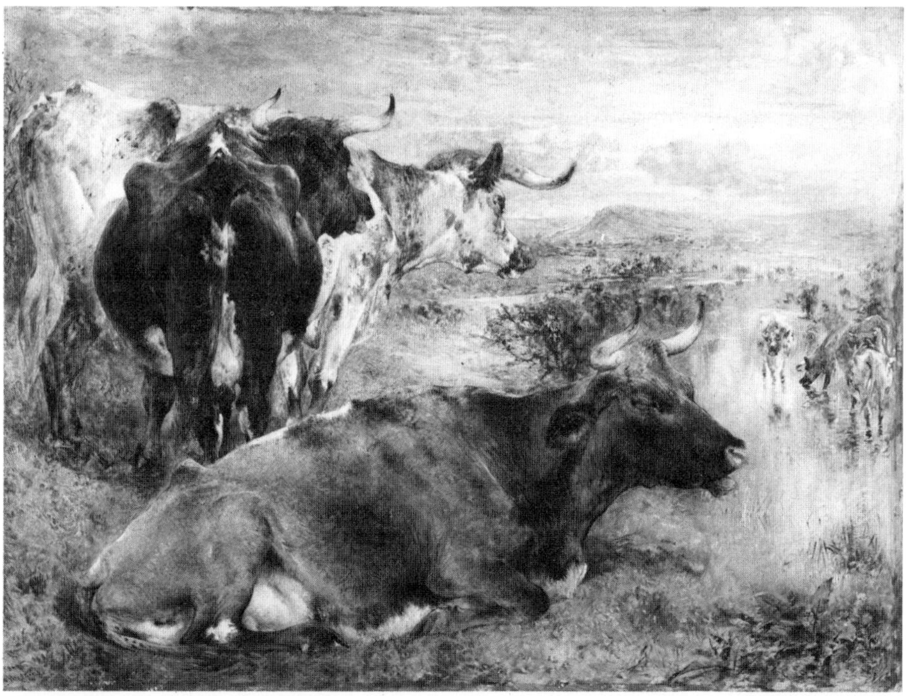

William Huggins
Cheshire Meadows
1868; oil on board, 46·7 × 62 cm
Walker Art Gallery, Liverpool

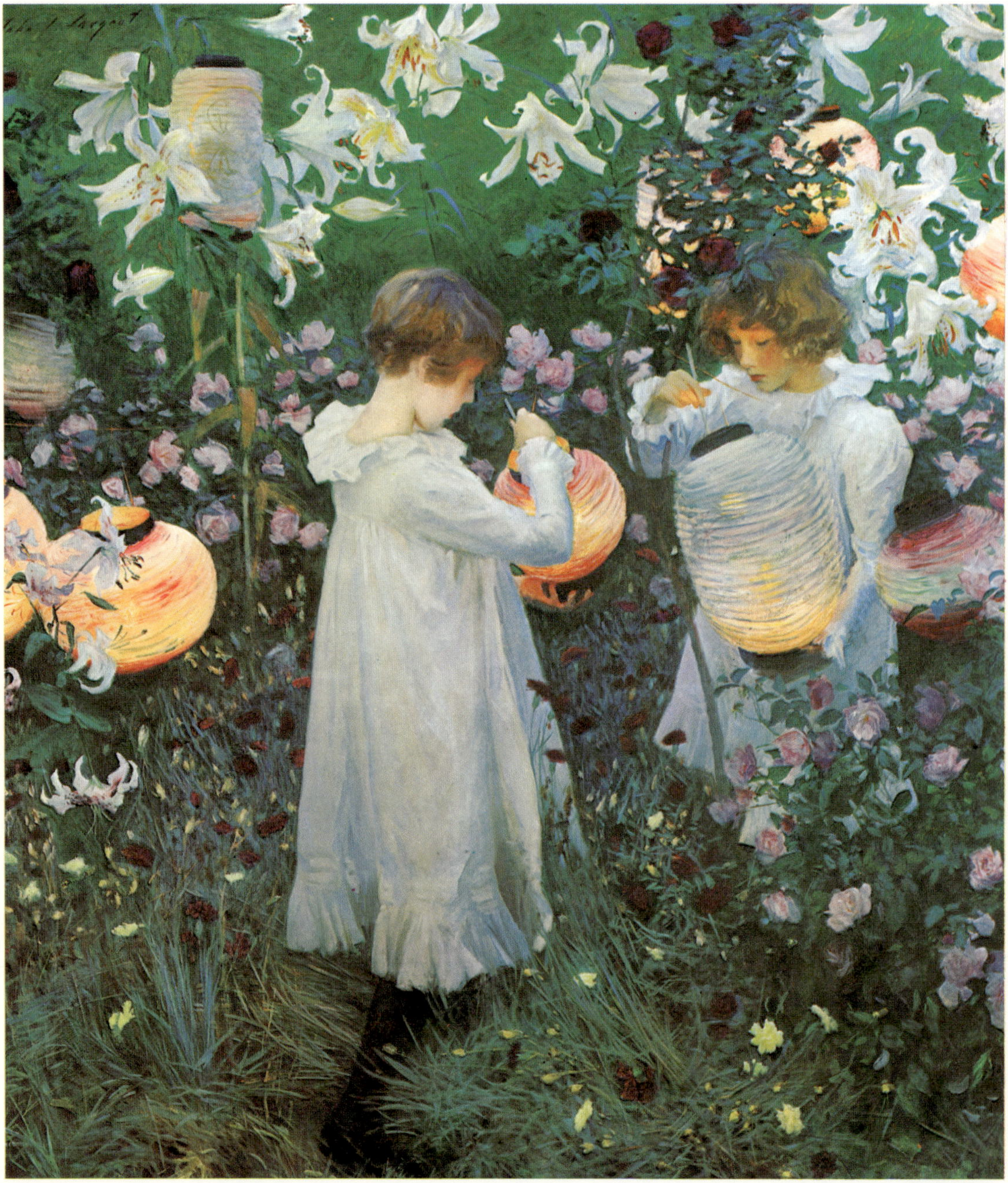

John Singer Sargent *Carnation, Lily, Lily, Rose* 1885–6; oil on canvas, 174× 153·7 cm Tate Gallery, London

William Huggins. He stayed here until the mid-1870s, when he moved for a short period to North Wales, returning in the early 1880s to settle at Christleton, where he died and is buried. His gravestone describes him as 'a just and compassionate man, who would neither tread on a worm nor cringe to an emperor'.

The Shrewsbury Arms Hotel at Mickle Trafford near Chester was the home of an aunt of Luke (later Sir Luke) Fildes, and he stayed here while a student at the School of Art in Warrington (then in the same building as the Museum), between 1860 and 1863.

Coleorton, *Leics.*

About fifteen miles north-east of Leicester stands Coleorton Hall, home from 1808 to his death in 1827 of the connoisseur Sir George Beaumont, much of whose collection of Old Masters went towards the setting up of the National Gallery. Beaumont was also a keen amateur painter and a generous patron, and many artists came to stay at Coleorton. Life here centred on Beaumont's first-floor Painting Room, where he would work side by side with guests such as David Wilkie and Benjamin Robert Haydon, who came to Coleorton together in 1809. Haydon's diary describes how they 'did nothing morning, noon or night but think of painting, talk of painting, dream of painting and wake to paint again'.

Beaumont believed in the classical tradition of landscape represented by Claude and Richard Wilson. This seemed to him to be giving way in the work of newcomers like Turner to 'pea-green insipidity'; he was, however, friendly towards Constable, perhaps feeling he had more chance of influencing him. The two men first met in 1795 in 'Constable's Country' itself, Beaumont's mother having settled at Dedham after her second marriage. They remained in contact throughout Constable's career, and in 1823 he came to spend six weeks at Coleorton. Constable's biographer outlines the kind of discussions on art he and Beaumont had at that time: 'A constant communion with pictures the tints of which

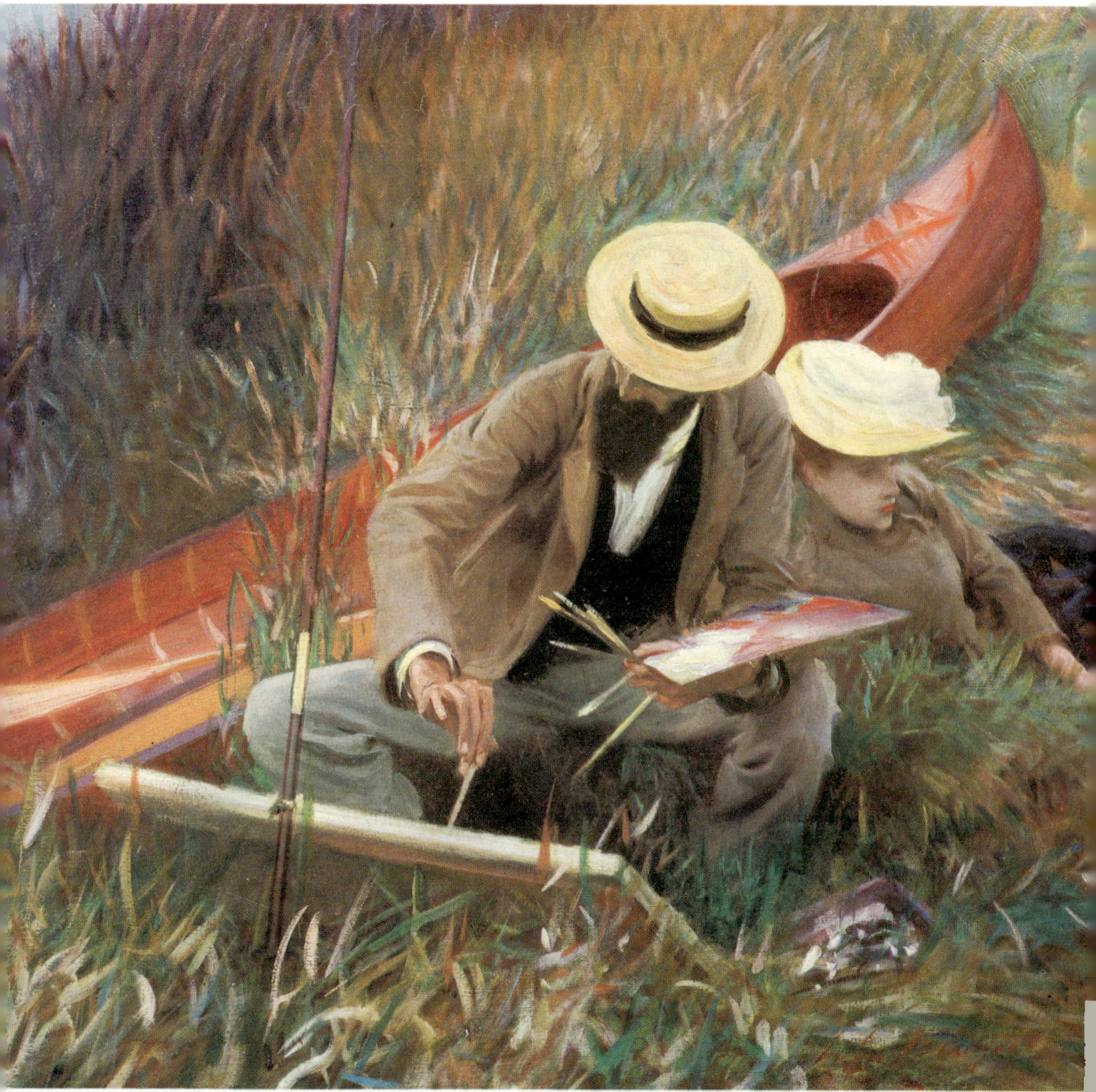

John Singer Sargent *Paul Helleu Sketching* (detail) 1889; oil on canvas, 66 × 81·3 cm Brooklyn Museum, New York

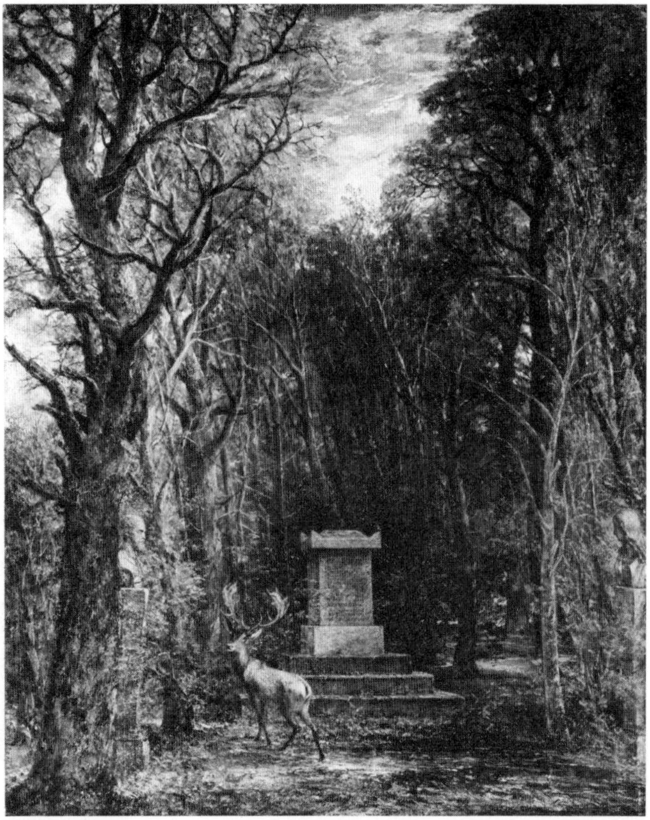

John Constable
The Cenotaph
1836; oil on canvas, 132 × 108·6 cm
National Gallery, London

OPPOSITE, ABOVE:
David Gee
Lady Godiva Procession
1867; oil on canvas, 76 × 63·5 cm
Herbert Art Gallery and Museum, Coventry

BELOW: Joseph Wright of Derby
Landscape with Dale Abbey
c. 1785; oil on canvas, 72·4 × 99 cm
Graves Art Gallery, Sheffield

are subdued by time no doubt tends to unfit the eye for the enjoyment of freshness; and Sir George thought Constable too daring in the modes he adopted to obtain this quality; while Constable saw that Sir George often allowed himself to be deceived by the effects of time, of accident, and by the tricks that are, far oftener than is generally supposed, played by dealers, to give mellowness to pictures; and, in these matters, each was disposed to set the other right. . . . Sir George recommended the colour of an old Cremona fiddle for the prevailing tone of everything, and this Constable answered by laying an old fiddle on the green lawn before the house. Again, Sir George, who seemed to consider the autumnal tints necessary, at least to some part of a landscape, said, "Do you not find it very difficult to determine where to place your *brown tree*?" And the reply was, "Not in the least, for I never put such a thing into a picture."'

In 1812 Beaumont had erected a commemorative stone to the great friend and mentor of his youth, Sir Joshua Reynolds. Constable made sketches of the sacred grove at Coleorton in which this monument stood (and still stands) and used them some years later for a major oil he called *The Cenotaph*. The inscription on the stone is by another of Beaumont's friends, Wordsworth. It ends:

. . . Yet here may I
Unblamed, upon my patrimonial grounds
Raise this frail tribute to his memory,
An humble follower of the soothing art
That he professed; attached to him in heart,
Admiring, loving, and with grief and pride,
Feeling what England lost when Reynolds died.

Coleorton was altered in 1862 with the addition of a second storey. More recently, the main rooms have been divided up into offices by the National Coal Board, which has owned the house since 1948. Many examples of Beaumont's work as an artist can be seen at Leicester Art Gallery.

Coventry, *West Midlands*

The most notable artist associated with Coventry before recent times was David Gee. He was born here in 1793, attended a local charity school, and, before taking up art as a fulltime profession, worked for a while in his father's watchmaking business. Like many provincial painters he had to be versatile, tackling inn-signs, banners and heraldic coach-painting as well as landscapes, portraits, and pictures of local events such as the annual Lady Godiva procession. For most of his life Gee lived in a house on the north side of Spon Street, near the junction with Barras Lane (gone). His work is well represented in the collection of the Herbert Art Gallery.

Coventry was the early home of John Skelton, the sculptor. He attended Bablake School and the local school of art, but now lives in Sussex. There are several examples of his work in Coventry, including a relief map of the city in the Trinity Street branch of Sainsbury's.

Derby, *Derbys.*

Joseph Wright of Derby was the son of an attorney; he was born in 1734 at 28 Irongate (the site, now No. 34, is marked with a plaque), where he spent most of his early life. After training in London, Wright worked throughout his twenties as a provincial portraitist, serving important families all over the Midlands. Dissatisfied with this way of life, he began in the 1760s to paint large subject-pictures that combined his interests in scientific demonstrations and dramatic chiaroscuro. Two of these, *A Philosopher Lecturing on the Orrery* and *An Experiment on a Bird in the Air Pump*, are probably the works by which he is best known today. His outdoor scenes show the same fascination with the effects of artificial light.

In 1773 Wright of Derby went for a two-year visit to Italy and, on returning, attempted without great success to take over the portrait practice recently vacated by Gainsborough in Bath. By 1777 he was back in Derby. He stayed initially in lodgings, but in 1779 bought St Helen's House on Duffield Road (the present St Helen's House, built on the same site, contains the offices of the County Borough of Derby Education Committee); here he lived until 1790, when he moved for the remaining seven years of his life to 26 Queen Street (gone). On returning from Italy, Wright's range of subject-matter extended to reveal a strong taste for themes of mortality like *The Indian Widow*. In addition, his feeling for landscape seems to have deepened, and his later work shows a new interest in capturing transient effects of nature. Derby Art Gallery contains twenty-eight of Wright's paintings and a large collection of drawings.

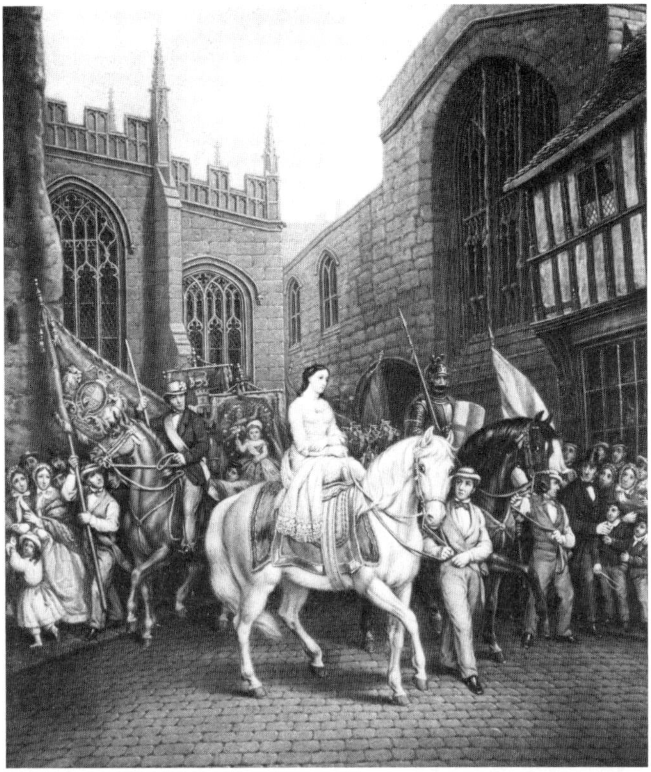

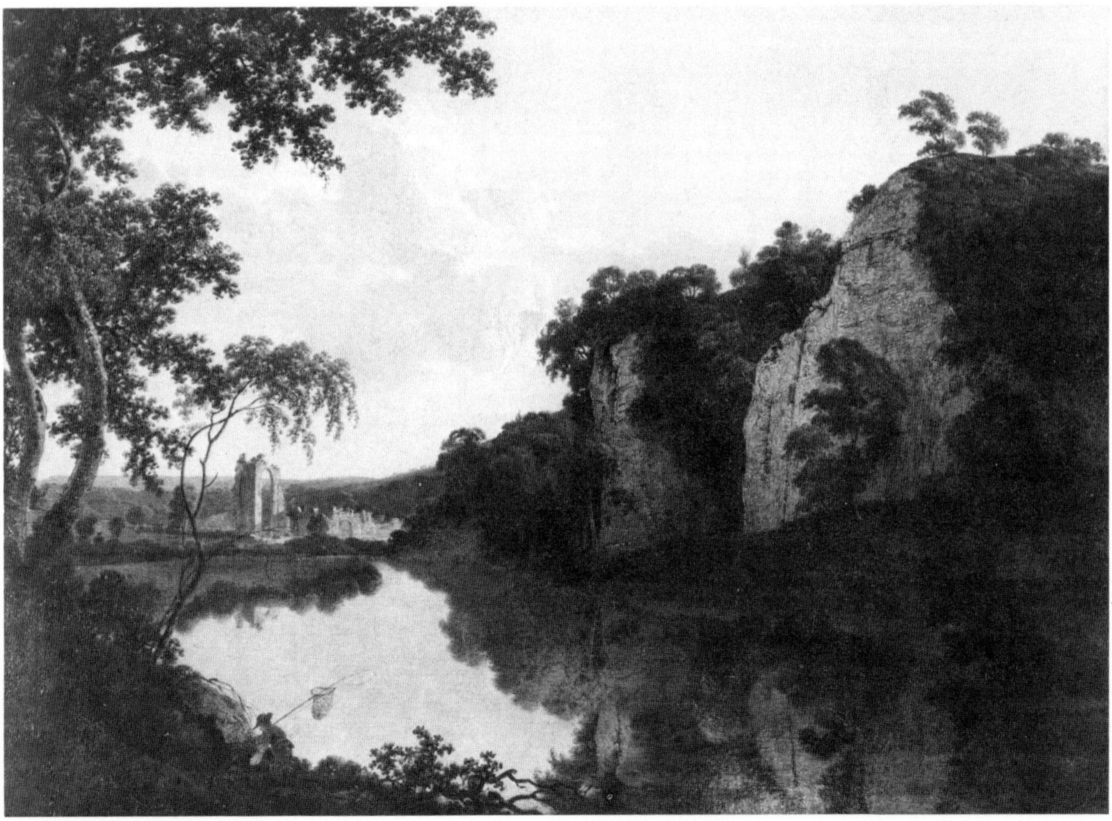

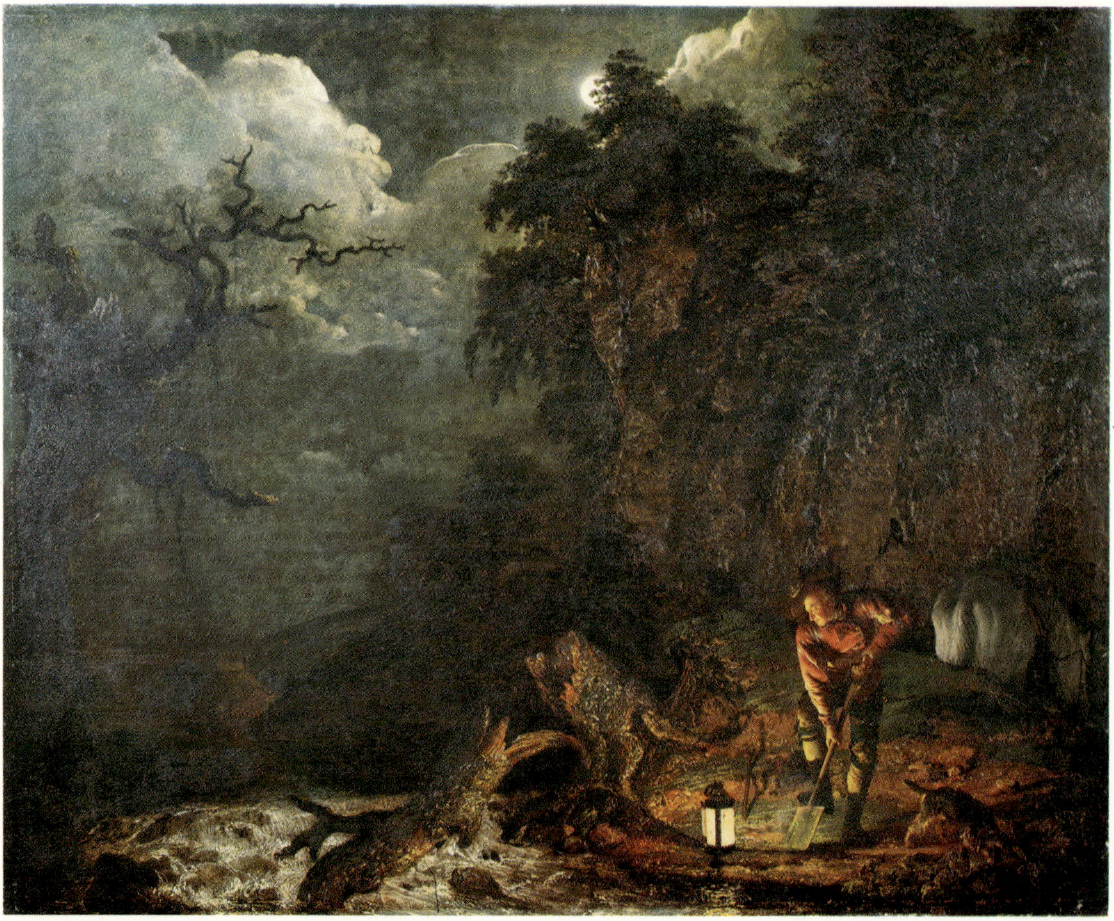

Joseph Wright of Derby
The Earthstopper on the Banks of the Derwent
1773; oil on canvas, 96·5 × 120·6 cm
Derby Art Gallery

Dudley, *West Midlands*

The little-known painter Percy Shakespeare was born in Dudley in 1906, the son of a local engineering fitter. He studied at the Dudley Art School, and later became a brilliant pupil at the Birmingham School of Art; but a German bomb put an end to his promising career in 1943.

Far Oakridge, *Glos.*

In the summer of 1912 William Rothenstein, his wife Alice and the Indian poet Rabindranath Tagore paid a visit to Gloucestershire. Walking together one afternoon along the Golden Valley, they came across an old and idyllically situated farmhouse. Although the building was in a very bad state of decay, the Rothensteins decided on impulse to buy it, together with its fifty-five acres of land. In the subsequent transformation of Iles farm, they created a home of outstanding beauty which left an unforgettable impression on all those who saw it. One visitor was Sir Francis Darwin, who afterwards wrote in a letter to Alice: 'I have never seen a more romantic house than yours – something in the way it stands, facing the valley, affected me so strangely, and I cannot say why – it felt to me like some place I had seen in a dream.'

After the Rothensteins had bought their house at Far Oakridge, William was reluctant to leave the area for any length of time. They gave up the farm in 1922, but moved two years later to a nearby cottage. William was obsessed by Far Oakridge, and painted Iles Farm and its surroundings on countless occasions. He also liked to portray the local villagers, and particularly those who practised traditional country crafts. A favourite subject was 'Eli the Thatcher', of whom he once gave a very vivid description: 'One old man, Eli Gardiner, noted hedger and thatcher, had the wisdom of the unlettered. He knew his Bible, the Old Testament especially, and could interpret the signs of the skies – the sun, clouds, and the flight of birds – and he knew the secret life of field and hedgerow.' When Rothenstein died in 1946, his body was carried to

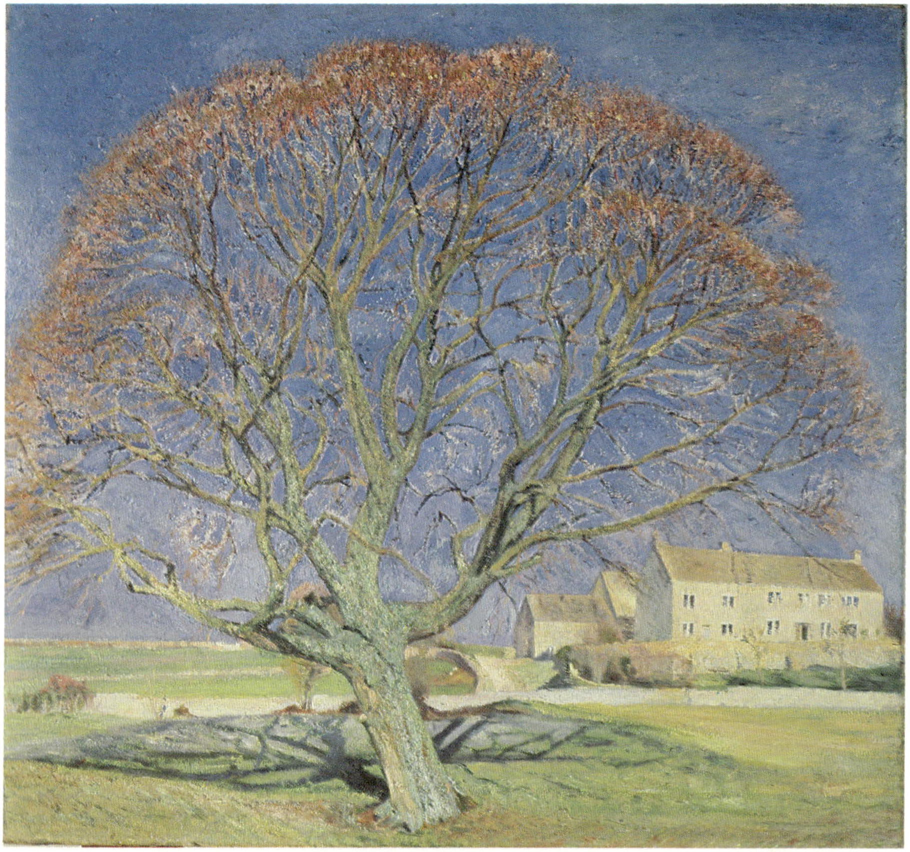

William
Rothenstein
St Martin's Summer
1915; oil on canvas,
84·4 × 91·8 cm
Manchester City
Art Gallery

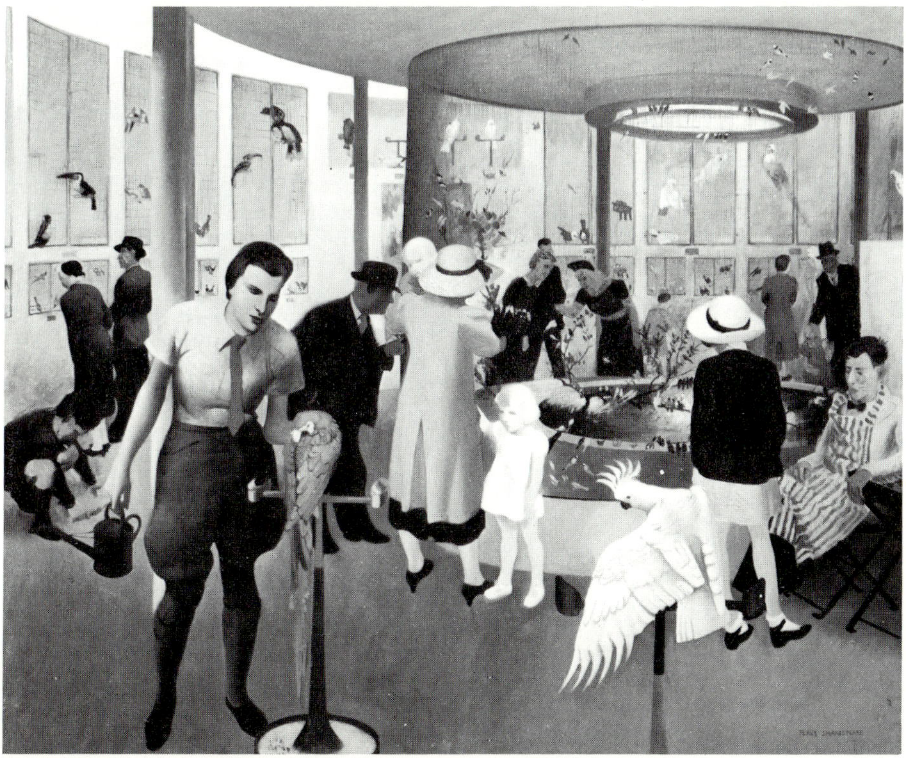

Percy Shakespeare
The Bird House,
Dudley Zoo
c. 1939; oil on
canvas, 76 × 92 cm
Collection of the
Misses M. and G.
Shakespeare

William Rothenstein
Eli the Thatcher
1913; oil on canvas, 76·5 × 63·3 cm
Manchester City Art Gallery

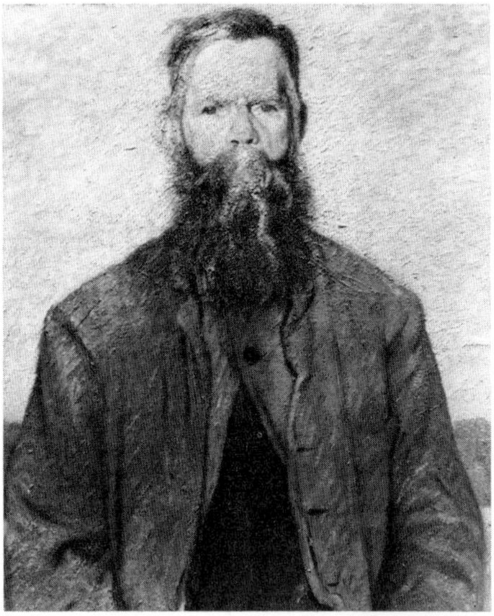

the local church of St Bartholomew in a farm-cart drawn by four of the local craftsmen whose portraits he had painted; he was buried at the foot of the church tower.

Garsington, *Oxon.*

Garsington Manor was from 1915 to 1927 the home of Lady Ottoline Morrell, who offered unflagging hospitality to a large number of young writers and artists. Among the many painters who stayed here were Augustus John, Henry Lamb, Gilbert Spencer, Dora Carrington and Mark Gertler, who looked upon Lady Morrell as a second mother. Sometimes the influx of guests was so great that rooms or studios had to be found in the village. During the First World War Garsington aroused considerable suspicion as a pacifist centre.

Mark Gertler
The Pond at Garsington
1916; oil on canvas, 63·3 × 63·3 cm
Leeds City Art Galleries

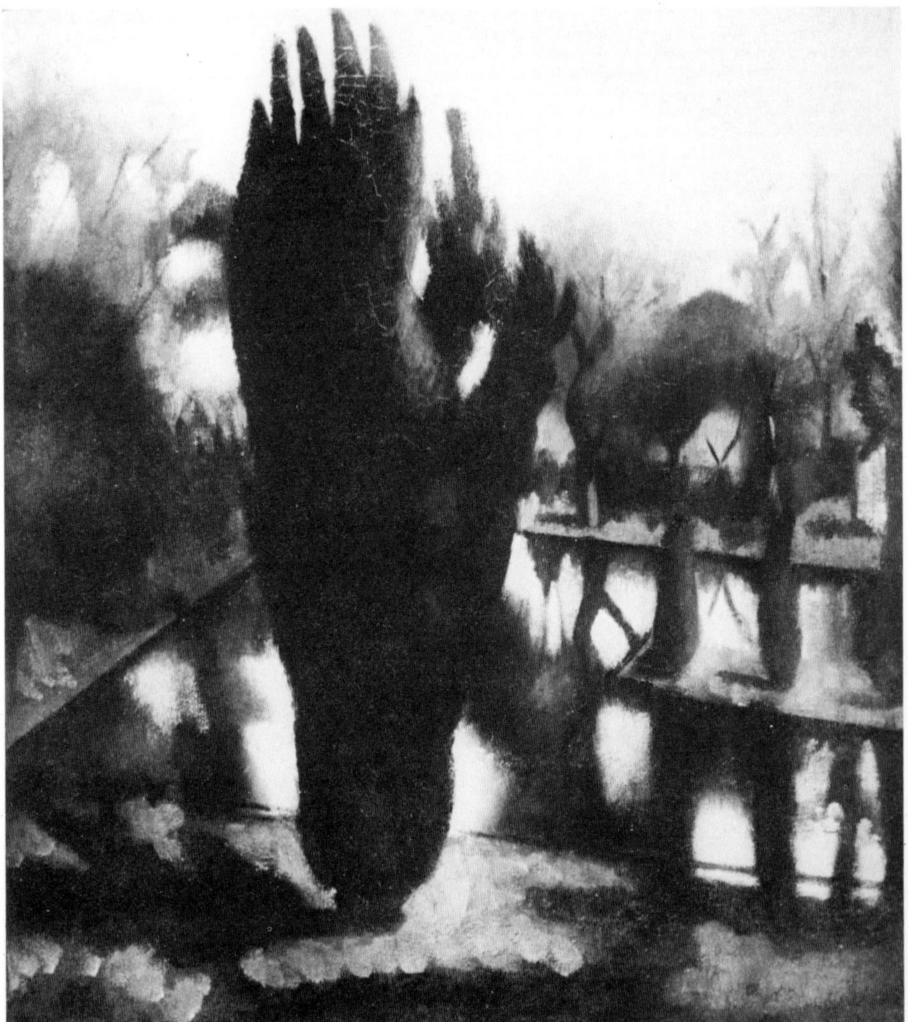

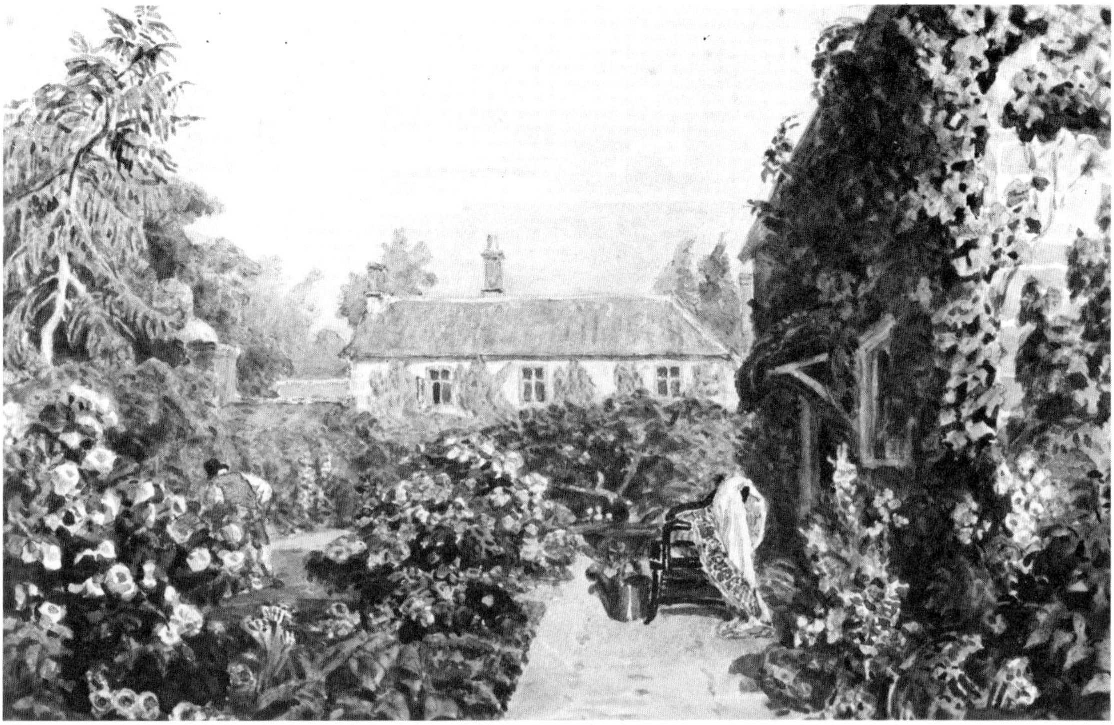

Joshua Cristall
The Artist's House and Garden at Goodrich
After 1821; watercolour, 16 × 25·3 cm
Dyer Collection

Gloucester, *Glos.*

Philip Wilson Steer, the English Impressionist, was a student at the Gloucester School of Art between 1878 and 1881. At first he commuted from his parents' home in Whitchurch (q.v.), then he took lodgings in Parliament Street; finally his mother joined him in the city and they lived together just a stone's throw from the School at 23 Brunswick Road (now St Michael's House). The portrait of its Principal, John Kemp, that Steer painted at this time still hangs in the School, which is now the Gloucestershire College of Art.

Goodrich, *Hereford and Worcester*

The pretty village of Goodrich was for twenty years the home of the watercolourist Joshua Cristall. He retreated here from London in 1822, at the age of fifty-four, under the friendly persuasion and assistance of Samuel Rush Meyrick, the wealthy antiquarian who was soon to build the fantasy-Gothic Goodrich Court (gone). The classical theme of the pastoral had been a recurrent one throughout Cristall's art, and in Goodrich he found its realization, just as Samuel Palmer found his 'Valley of Vision' in Shoreham during the same decade. Cristall was a keen gardener and spent much of his time cultivating the small plot of land attached to his house, Granton Cottage (now much altered). As well as his luxuriant garden, he often painted the yearly cutting and burning of bracken on Coppet Hill; other favourite sites, in which he saw intimations of Arcadia, were Coldwell Rocks and Symond's Yat.

Hereford, *Hereford and Worcester*

Towards the end of 1814 an advertisement for a drawing-master appeared in *The Times*. The terms proposed were £100 per annum to teach twice a week in a ladies' school run by a Miss Croucher in Hereford. David Cox, who was then living in London, saw the advertisement and was attracted to the post because of the easy access from Hereford to favourite sketching sites in the Wye Valley and North Wales, and also the lower cost of living in the country. He applied and was appointed. In addition to instructing the ladies at Miss Croucher's establishment (now the Farmer's Club in Widemarsh Street), Cox taught boys at the Grammar School and also gave private lessons. Most notable among his pupils were his own son, who attended the Grammar School and went on to be an artist in his own right, and Joseph Murray Ince, the landscape, marine and architectural painter who lived most of his life in Presteigne, just over the Welsh border.

David Cox
Butchers' Row, Hereford
1815; watercolour, 42·4×52 cm
Hereford City Museum

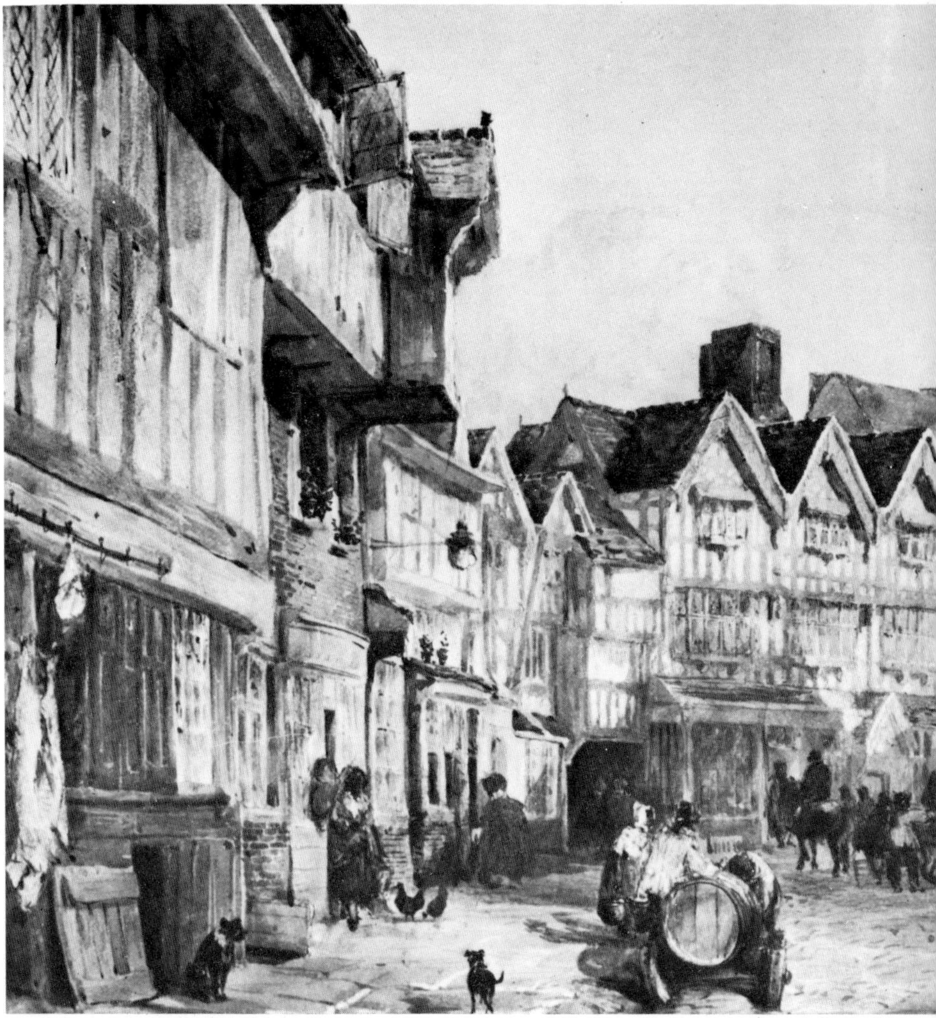

Initially, Cox rented an old cottage outside the city in Lower Lyde, but he soon moved to George Cottage (gone) on the north side of Ayleston Hill, where he remained for two years. Between 1817 and 1824 he lived in a picturesque thatched cottage then known as Parry's Cottage and now No. 42 Venns Lane, and between 1824 and 1827 he occupied the somewhat larger Ash Tree House (gone) which he built for himself, again on Ayleston Hill. In 1827 he left Hereford to return to London.

At the turn of this century Hereford produced an artist of outstanding early promise in Brian Hatton. Hatton was born in 1887 at Carlton Villas, Whitecross Road, and in 1895 his family moved to Mount Craig, Broomy Hill. He was an infant prodigy, and drew with total proficiency by the age of thirteen. The painter G. F. Watts was convinced of his genius and, when Hatton was sixteen, wrote about him to his mother in the most glowing terms: 'Nature has endowed him in an extraordinary manner and he may – should! – become the greatest artist England has had. . . . I want you to feel that nothing but serious accident bars his way to the highest place, there is nothing that anyone can teach and nothing for him but to observe and think. . . .' Not surprisingly, Hatton was greatly pampered, and when he fell ill on one occasion Watts's wife telegraphed daily to his parents for the latest bulletin.

Hatton's precocity was largely limited to draughtsmanship, and when he visited St Ives in his teens, the colony of artists there considered his colour-sense to be wanting. More seriously, he appears to have been lacking in imagination, and his subject-matter rarely extended beyond horse-scenes. At nineteen he went to study at Hospitalfield in Arbroath, but was soon expelled on account of uncharacteristically

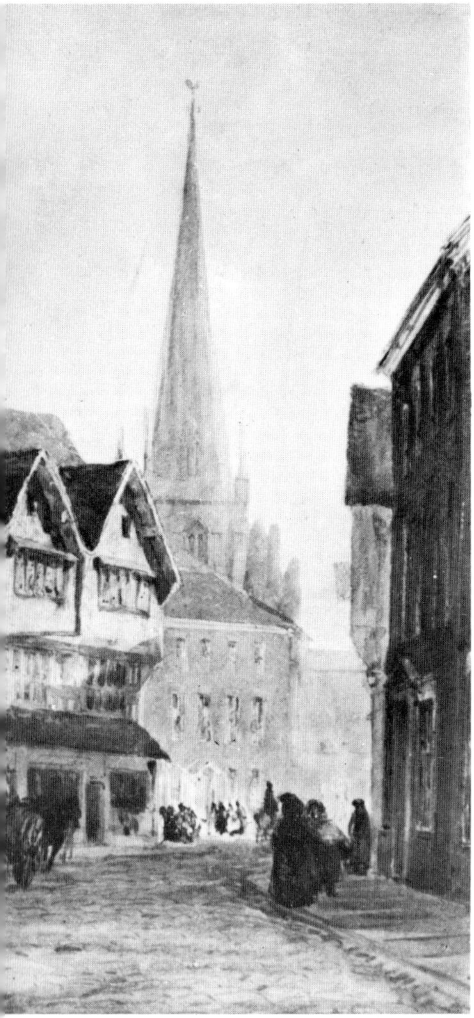

rowdy behaviour. In 1909 the artist started working professionally in the converted coach-house of his family's home in Hereford. During the First World War he was stationed in Egypt with the Worcestershire Yeomanry, and after one battle wrote back enthusiastically to his parents: 'I thoroughly enjoyed myself. . . . One only has to take reasonable precautions and lie down behind a few inches of sand hill to be quite safe from any bullet.' He was killed thirteen days later. Members of his family devoted much energy to preserving his memory in the city of his birth, and in 1973 a gallery in the Churchill Gardens Museum was dedicated to him.

Horkstow, *Humberside*

This remote village, then in Lincolnshire, was the home of George Stubbs during the most crucial period of his career, the eighteen months in 1758–9 that he devoted to research into the anatomy of the horse. According to local tradition, he and his mistress Mary Spencer lived at Hall Farm (now divided into two cottages and much altered), near the now derelict Horkstow Hall; he presumably performed his gruesome dissections in a nearby barn. For this purpose, horses would be bled to death and their arteries and veins injected with some hardening substance. The carcass would then be suspended from the ceiling by iron hooks and Stubbs would dissect it, recording details with greater precision than any other animal anatomist had done before him. Each horse occupied six or seven weeks' work. Stubbs's findings were published in 1766 as *The Anatomy of the Horse*. The drawings made at Horkstow, which served as illustrations to the book and were later in Edwin Landseer's collection, are now at the Royal Academy. They were the starting point of Stubbs's career as an animal-painter, and have earned him the reputation of greatest artist-scientist after Leonardo da Vinci.

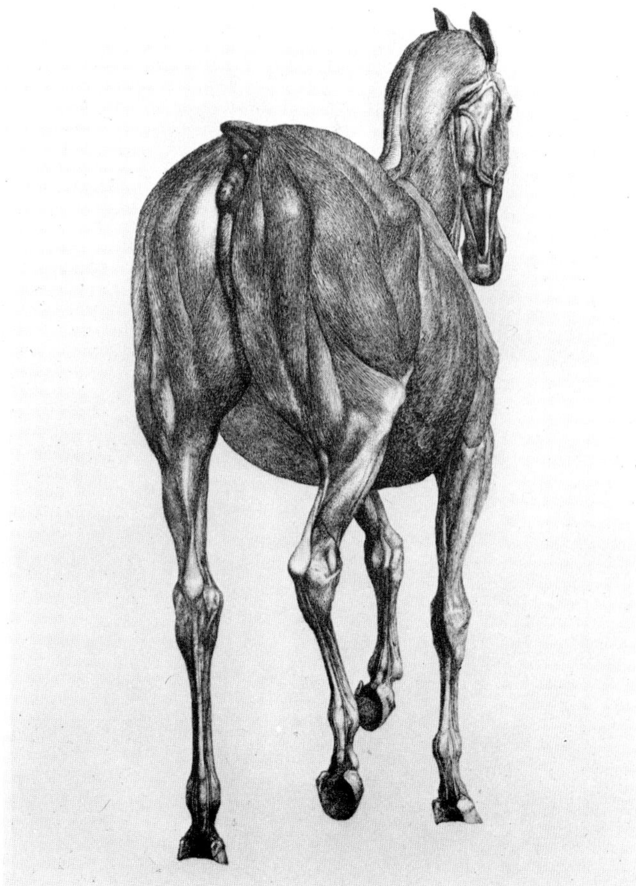

George Stubbs
Table XII from *The Anatomy of the Horse*
1766
Royal Academy of Arts, London

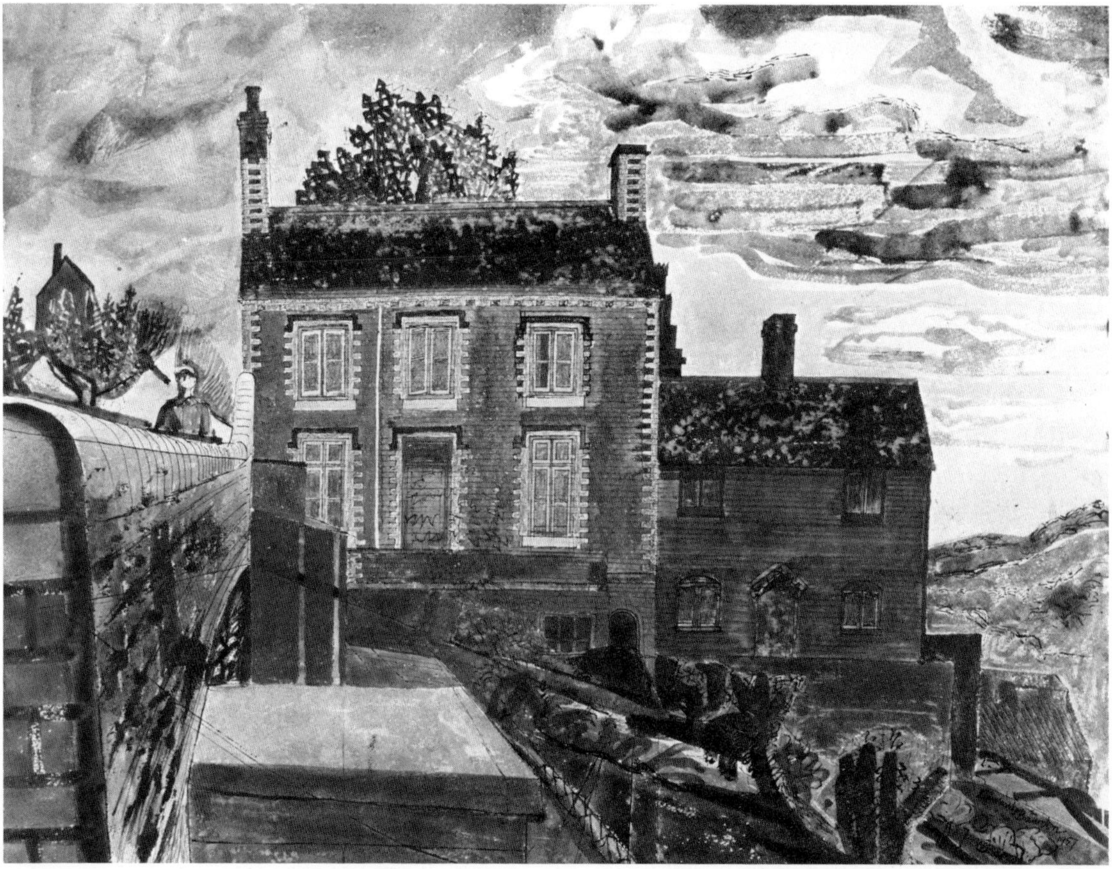

Edward Bawden
Houses at Ironbridge
1956; pen, ink and watercolour,
47×58·4 cm
Tate Gallery, London

Ironbridge, *Salop*

The early industrial site of Ironbridge Gorge (now an open-air museum complex) was an attraction for travelling artists from around 1750 onwards; between that date and 1830 as many as fifty are known to have visited the area. This was due both to its convenient situation on the tourist route to North Wales from London and to its unique combination of romantic scenery and spectacular industrial workings. The dramatic lighting effects created by lime kilns and ironworks provided subjects for Turner, Cotman and Paul Sandby Munn. But the most familiar image of the gorge is P. J. de Loutherbourg's *Coalbrookdale by Night*. This shows the view looking eastwards along the north bank of the Severn, with Bedlam furnaces on the right (these are currently being excavated) and hellish flames and smoke coming from some coke-hearths behind them; the buildings on the left were demolished in the 1830s, but the roadway followed by the cart in the foreground survives as part of Waterloo Street.

In September and October 1956 Edward Bawden spent six weeks at Ironbridge, where he was joined by John Aldridge, John Nash and Carel Weight; they all painted views of the area, but were especially attracted by the bridge.

Kelmscott, *Oxon.*

In 1871 William Morris and Dante Gabriel Rossetti took the joint tenancy of Kelmscott Manor, a sixteenth-century house near the Thames a few miles above Lechlade. They spent much time together here over the next three years, Rossetti coming mainly to enjoy the company of his favourite model, Morris's beautiful wife Jane; indeed she was the idol of his life at this time. Inevitably a certain amount of tension grew up between the two men and from 1874 Rossetti discontinued his visits to the place, allowing the whole tenancy to pass to Morris. The manor remained Morris's summer retreat until his death in 1896 and a woodcut of it was used as a frontispiece for his Utopian story *News from Nowhere* (1891). It now belongs to the Society of Antiquaries of London and is open to the public on certain days of the year.

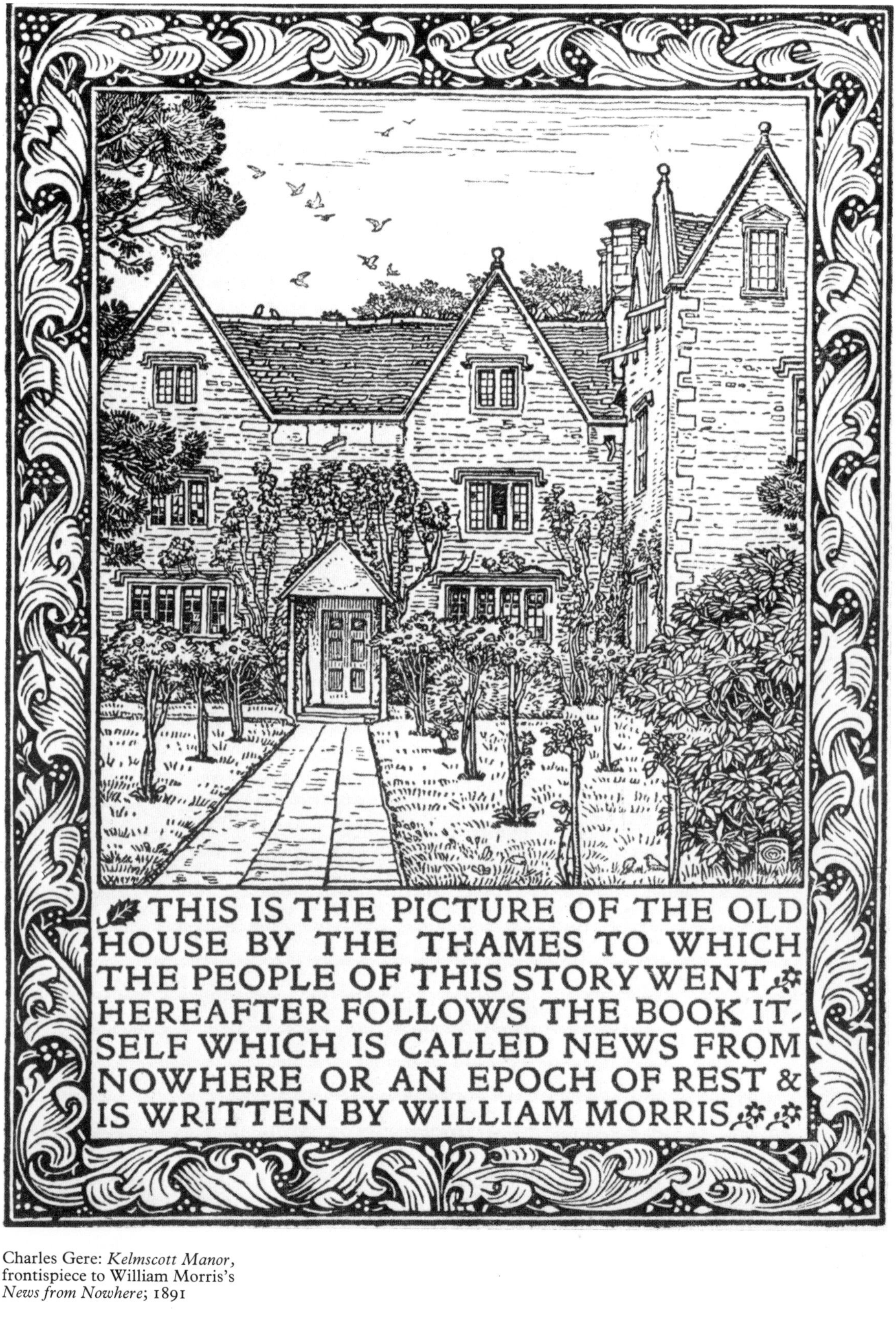

Charles Gere: *Kelmscott Manor*, frontispiece to William Morris's *News from Nowhere*; 1891

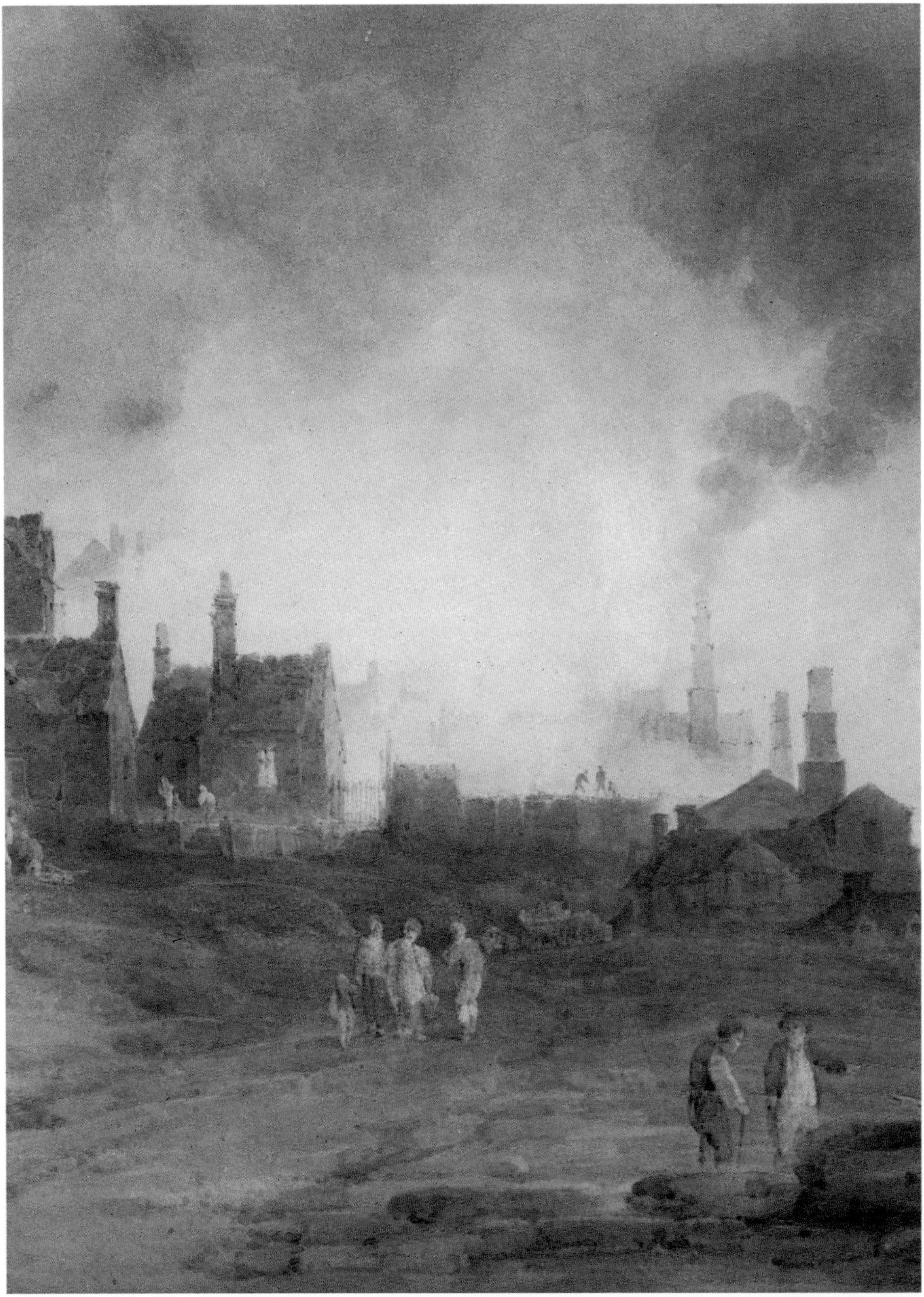

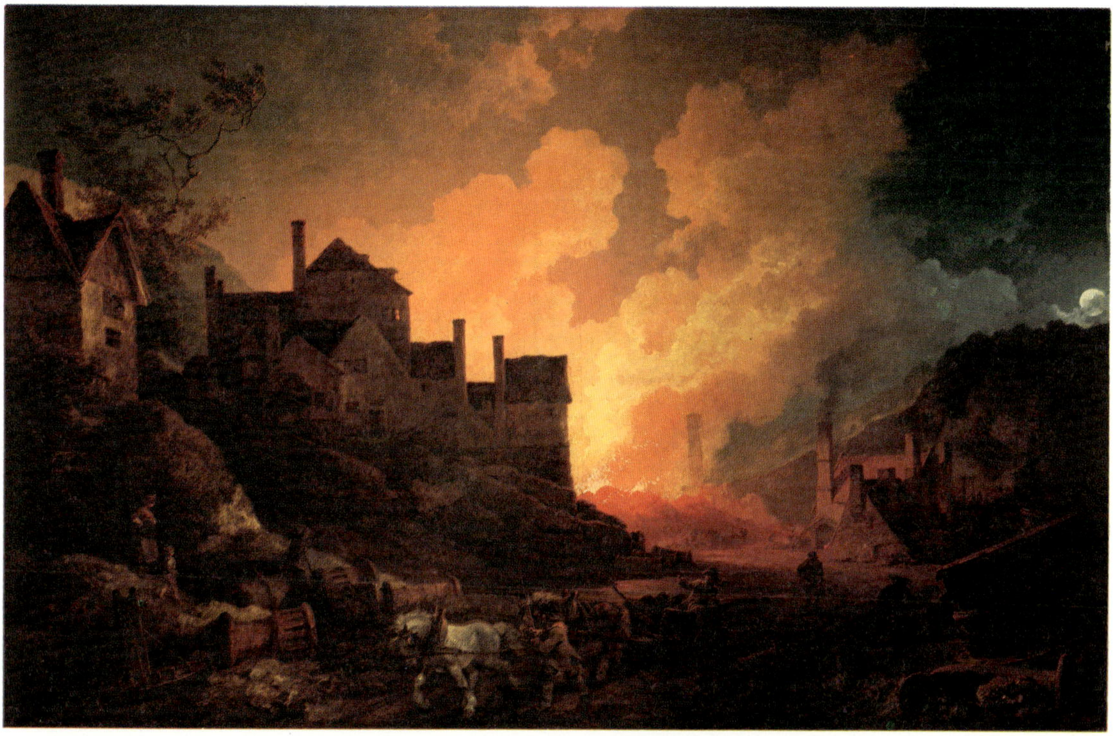

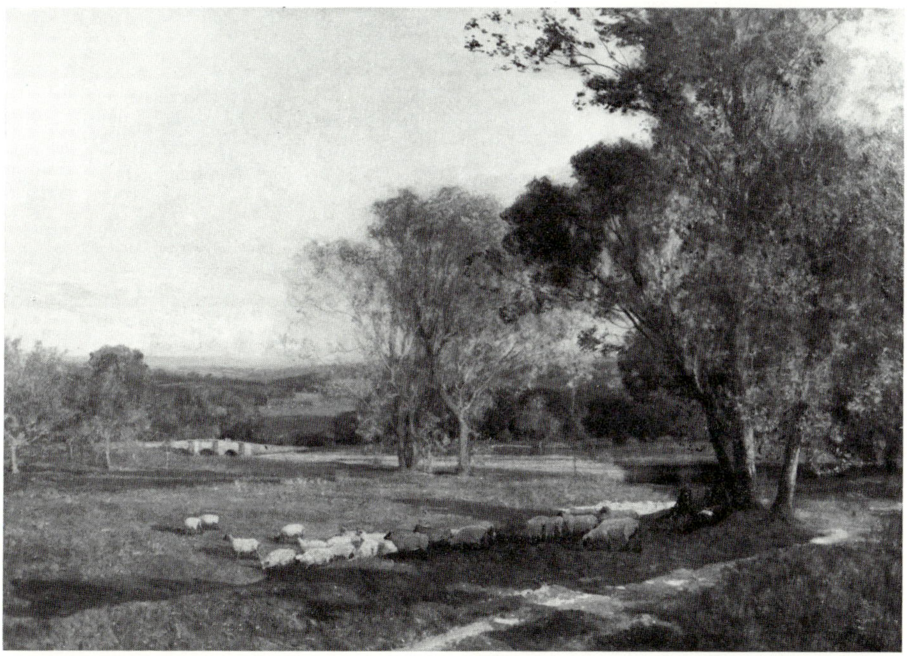

P. J. de Loutherbourg *Coalbrookdale by Night* 1801; oil on canvas, 68 × 106·7 cm Science Museum, London

Alfred East *Midland Meadows* Oil on canvas, 156 × 218 cm Alfred East Art Gallery, Kettering

OPPOSITE: Paul Sandby Munn *Bedlam Furnace* (detail) 1803; watercolour, 32·4 × 55 cm Collection of Judy Egerton, London

Kettering, *Northants.*

The Victorian landscapist Alfred East was born in Lower Street in Kettering (house gone) and the local art gallery in Sheep Street is named after him and contains a large collection of his work. East's near-contemporary and fellow native of Kettering was Thomas Cooper Gotch, who is best known as a painter of children. Gotch's family home was the Mission House in Lower Street and he attended Kettering Grammar School, although most of his working life was spent in Cornwall.

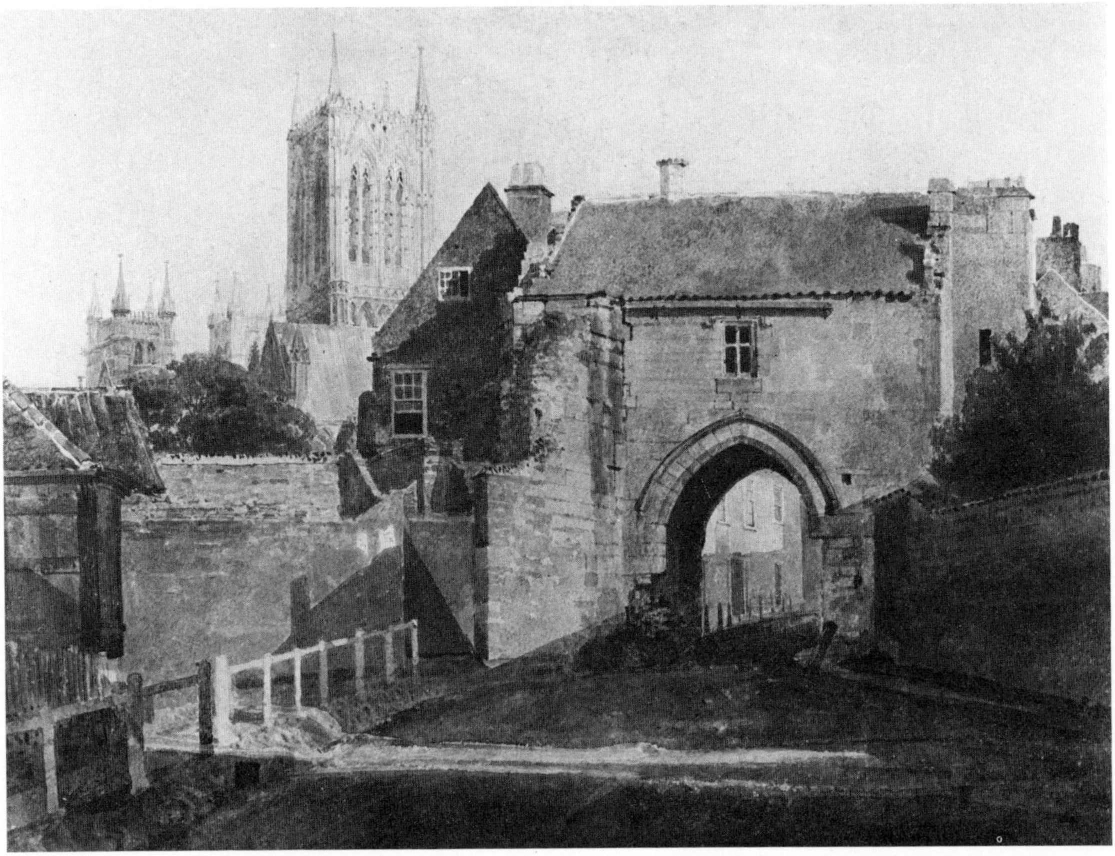

Peter de Wint
Pottergate, Lincoln
Watercolour,
29 × 39·7 cm
Victoria and Albert
Museum, London

Lichfield, *Staffs.*

John Glover was born in 1767 at Houghton-on-the-Hill just outside Leicester; by 1794 he was working as a teacher of drawing and painting in Lichfield and lived here for the next ten years. He was greatly influenced by the classical landscape tradition and was called 'our Lichfield Claude' by the local poet Anna Seward. He left the city in 1805 and spent twenty-five years painting and exhibiting his work in London, but his most interesting pictures are the landscapes he painted in Tasmania after emigrating there in 1830.

Lincoln, *Lincs.*

Peter de Wint, the landscapist, was born at Stone in Staffordshire in 1784. He came to know Lincoln through an artist friend he met while training in London. This was William Hilton, whose parents lived here and whose sister de Wint fell in love with and married. In 1814 the couple bought a house near the cathedral, on the corner of Drury Lane and Union Road (now marked with a plaque). They divided their time between Lincoln and another house in London for the next thirty years, and de Wint made many watercolours and paintings of local views.

An interesting but almost forgotten figure of later nineteenth-century British art is William Tom Warrener, who came from a prominent Lincoln family. He was born here in 1861, studied at the local school of art, and later settled in Paris, where he became a friend and follower of Toulouse-Lautrec. Lautrec made several portraits of him and featured him in a poster design as *L'Anglais au Moulin Rouge*. In 1906 Warrener returned to Lincoln to take over the family coal-merchant business and did relatively little painting after that date. He lived at St Margaret's Lodge in Upper Lindum Street until his death in 1934.

Lypiatt Park, *Glos.*

Lypiatt Park, a Victorian mansion in the Cotswolds, has been the home since 1957 of the sculptor Lynn Chadwick. Its castellated and pinnacled architecture forms a sympathetic setting for Chadwick's work, itself strongly Gothic in flavour.

Newark, *Notts.*

Sir William Nicholson was born in Newark at 12 London Road (plaque) in 1872; he was the son of a well-to-do industrialist who owned an ironworks specializing in agricultural machinery. William's father was a very stern and upright man, conscious of his social status (the Nicholson emblem was affixed to one of the ceilings of the London Road house) and devoutly religious; in 1880 he became Conservative Member of Parliament for Newark. Nicholson was sent to the Magnus School in Newark, and although this building was only a few hundred yards away from his home, his father insisted that he should attend as a boarder. Nicholson was so unhappy at this place that the prospect of returning after the summer holidays prompted him on one occasion to attempt suicide by swallowing two glasses of stagnant water from a garden well.

For Nicholson the only fortunate consequence of having attended the Magnus School was to have had a drawing-master who immediately recognized his pupil's talents. This man, William Cubley (or 'Old Cubley', as he was known to the boys), was an unexciting artist who specialized in topographical views (several of these are owned by the Newark Art Gallery). He nonetheless endeared himself to Nicholson by suggesting that he should be allowed to have private drawing lessons at home; in later life Nicholson painted his portrait, which he described as a 'very bad portrait of a very good man'. Nicholson matured rapidly as an artist and was soon commissioned by the local vicar to do a drawing of a font in the church. Eventually, in 1880 – again on the advice of Cubley – Nicholson applied to enter Herkomer's art school at Bushey in Hertfordshire; he was accepted, on his submission of a charcoal study of an old Newark woman, and remained at Bushey until 1890.

When Nicholson completed his period at art school, his father was anxious that he should not drift away from the family, and had a studio built for him in the garden of the London Road house. Nicholson worked here for a few months; but the lure of Paris proved greater than anything that Newark or family life could offer. He went to Paris in 1890, and thereafter never returned to live in the Midlands. Before his final departure from home Nicholson painted a portrait of his mother. This painting did not meet with his father's approval, and earned the angry remark: 'What is it? – but what is it?'

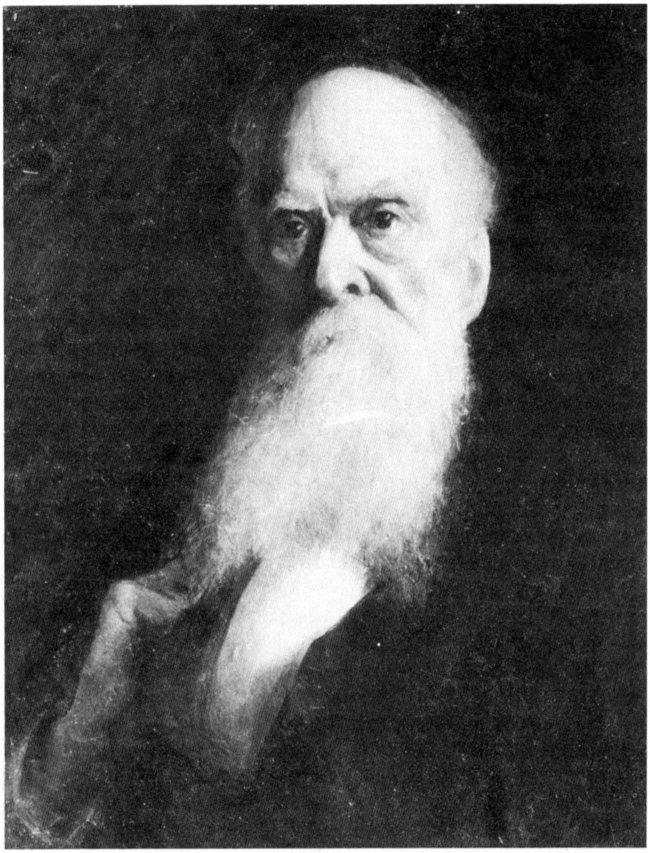

William Nicholson
William Cubley
Before 1895; oil on canvas, 61×48·3 cm
Castle Museum, Nottingham

Nottingham, *Notts.*

The present Labour Party Club in the High Street in Arnold was the birthplace of Richard Parkes Bonington (plaque). His father was a drawing-master and his mother ran a school. In 1818, when he was sixteen, the family went to live in Paris, the father having abandoned teaching in favour of a machine-exporting business. Bonington's short career (he died at twenty-five) was spent almost entirely in Paris, where for a time he shared a studio with his friend and admirer, Delacroix. He painted mainly landscapes and romantic historical subjects.

Dame Laura Knight was born at Long Eaton, but when she was two years old her family moved to Nottingham and settled at Ethel Villas, 9 Noel Street (plaque). The household in which she was brought up was an unusual one and the source of much local gossip. Her mother was estranged from a husband who had married her in the mistaken belief that her family, the Bates, were rich. They did in fact own a lace-machine factory in Nottingham, but Laura's grandfather, an inventor, had

OVERLEAF: John Everett Millais
James Wyatt and his Granddaughter
1849; oil on panel, 35·8×45·2 cm
Private collection

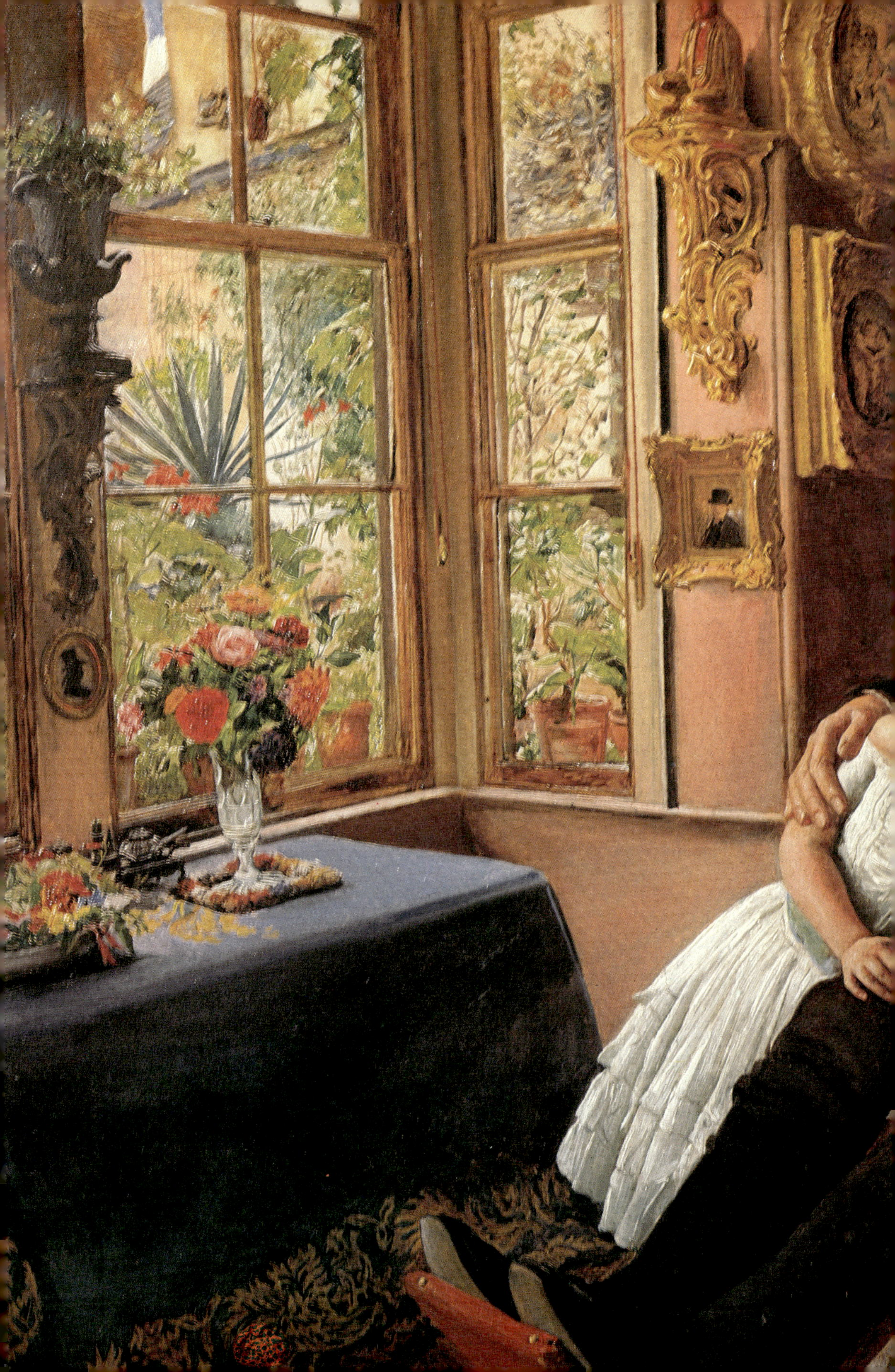

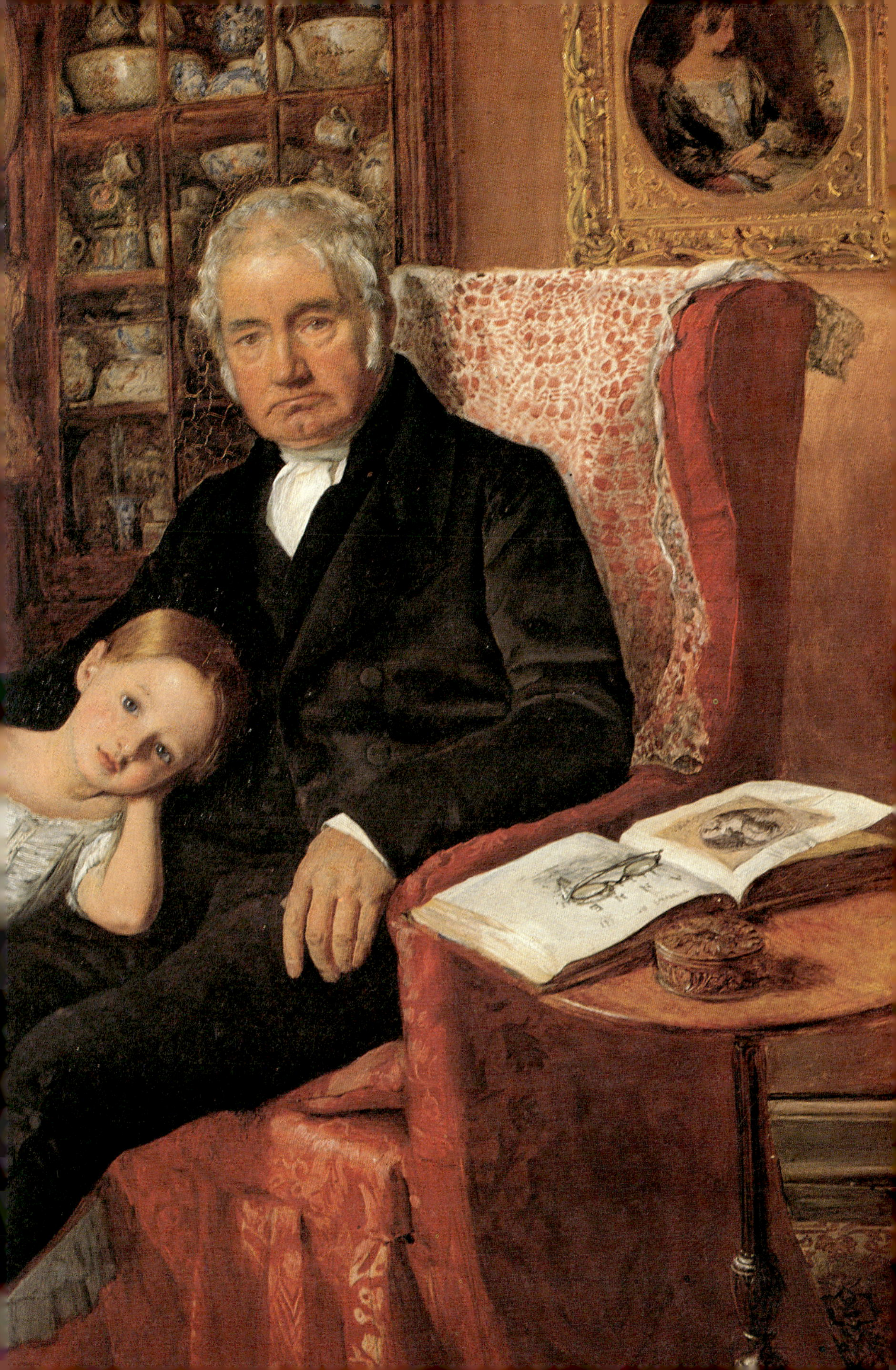

neglected to take out patents for his machines, and other people had been quick to plagiarize his ideas and undersell him. When he had died, his wife had taken over the running of this increasingly insecure firm, and she had come together with other members of the family to live at Ethel Villas. Worsening poverty forced the family subsequently to move to a smaller and cheaper house further down Noel Street (No. 35) and eventually to a workman's cottage near by.

Laura's mother, who was an art teacher and gave drawing lessons at her home, did everything to encourage her daughter's artistic talents. Lack of funds had prevented her from receiving a proper art education herself and she was determined that her daughter should not suffer in the same way. In 1890 the thirteen-year-old Laura was sent to the Nottingham School of Art. On almost her first day there Laura met her future husband Harold Knight, who was then the school's most talented student. Harold and Laura soon entered a rather diffident courtship which lasted, apparently on a purely platonic basis, for over thirteen years. Harold, whose father was a successful Nottingham architect, was temperamentally very different from Laura: he was a shy, reserved man who found Laura's ebullience and ceaseless chatter (generally about herself) rather overwhelming. Moreover his mother had instilled in him a strongly puritanical nature and a fear of sex. Harold was in many ways the more serious and dedicated artist, but Laura, who fell completely under his spell, even to the extent of imitating his works, had a more extrovert manner of painting, which was to win her greater public renown.

After leaving art school, Laura moved with her sister Nellie to a most unusual residence situated in a cave underneath Nottingham Castle. Laura had already begun to receive commissions for portraits, and she thought that by having such a distinctive and convenient address, at the edge of the city's most exclusive park, she would be able to attract more clients. The actual living conditions of the cave-dwelling – cold, damp, and infested with rats – turned out, however, to be less than desirable.

The first signs of official recognition for Laura's and Harold's work came in 1894; in that year they were awarded a gold and a silver medal respectively by the Prince of Wales. Later in the year Harold won a travelling scholarship and spent a period of eight months in Paris; his funds were insufficient, and when he called to see Laura at 'Castle Rooms' on his return, she was shocked by his bedraggled and emaciated appearance. Shortly afterwards an aunt of Laura's who lived in France arrived in Nottingham and suggested that they should both come with her to the holiday resort of Staithes on the Yorkshire coast. Both Laura and Harold liked Staithes so much that they lived there almost constantly for the next fourteen years. On a return visit to Nottingham in 1903, Laura submitted a work to the Royal Academy in London; it was accepted and later bought by the painter Edward Stott for the then princely sum of £20. The purchase of this work finally enabled Laura and Harold to marry; they returned to Staithes for a further seven years, then moved on to Newlyn, and finally settled in London.

BELOW:
Pre-Raphaelite Oxford

OPPOSITE, ABOVE:
William Holman Hunt
The Reverend J. D. Jenkins, New College Cloisters
1852; oil on panel, 35·6 × 25·4 cm
Jesus College, Oxford

OPPOSITE, BELOW:
Dante Gabriel Rossetti
Sir Launcelot's Vision of the Sanc Grael
1857; watercolour and bodycolour over black chalk, 68·6 × 104·1 cm
Ashmolean Museum, Oxford

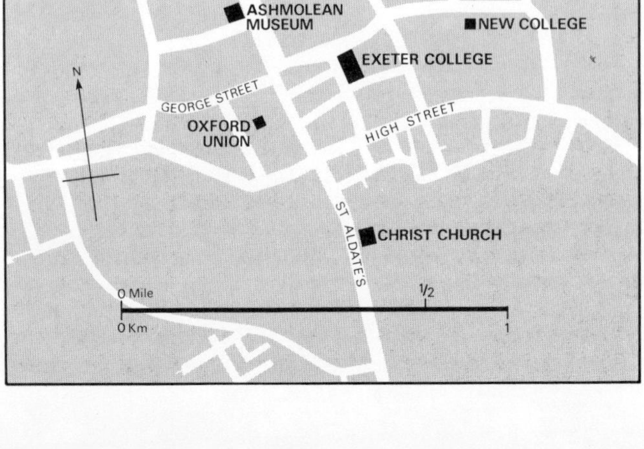

Oxford, *Oxon.*

John Everett Millais, one of the founder-members of the Pre-Raphaelite Brotherhood, had relatives in Oxford and was a regular visitor here as early as 1846, when he was seventeen. Around that date he became friendly with the local art dealer James Wyatt, who took an interest in his budding career and introduced him to patrons in the area such as James Drury, the eccentric occupant of Shotover Park. Wyatt himself bought a number of Millais's works and in 1849 commissioned a portrait of himself and his granddaughter, set in the back room of his house above his shop at

115 High Street (now a silversmith's). The work shows the unidealizing approach to portraiture and the minutely detailed treatment of nature that are characteristic of early Pre-Raphaelitism. At the same time Millais painted backgrounds in Oxford for certain of his subject-pictures, notably *The Woodman's Daughter* (Guildhall Art Gallery), most of which was painted at Botley.

Millais stayed with Wyatt in the summer of 1849 and returned for a further visit in the following year, during which he got to know Thomas Combe, Superintendent of the Clarendon Press. Soon afterwards Combe invited him to come and stay a few weeks at his house in the quadrangle of the Press. Millais introduced Combe to his friend and fellow Pre-Raphaelite Charles Collins, who also came to stay, and encouraged him to acquire Holman Hunt's picture of *A Converted British Family sheltering a Christian Priest from the Persecution of the Druids*, which was hanging unsold at the current Royal Academy exhibition. Combe did not actually buy this work himself – he had his wife's wealthy uncle make him a present of it – but he soon began to patronize the Pre-Raphaelites directly, and with great generosity. They in turn honoured him with nicknames, 'the Early Christian' and 'the Patriarch'. His collection is more or less intact in the form of the Combe Bequest of twenty-one paintings and drawings at the Ashmolean Museum.

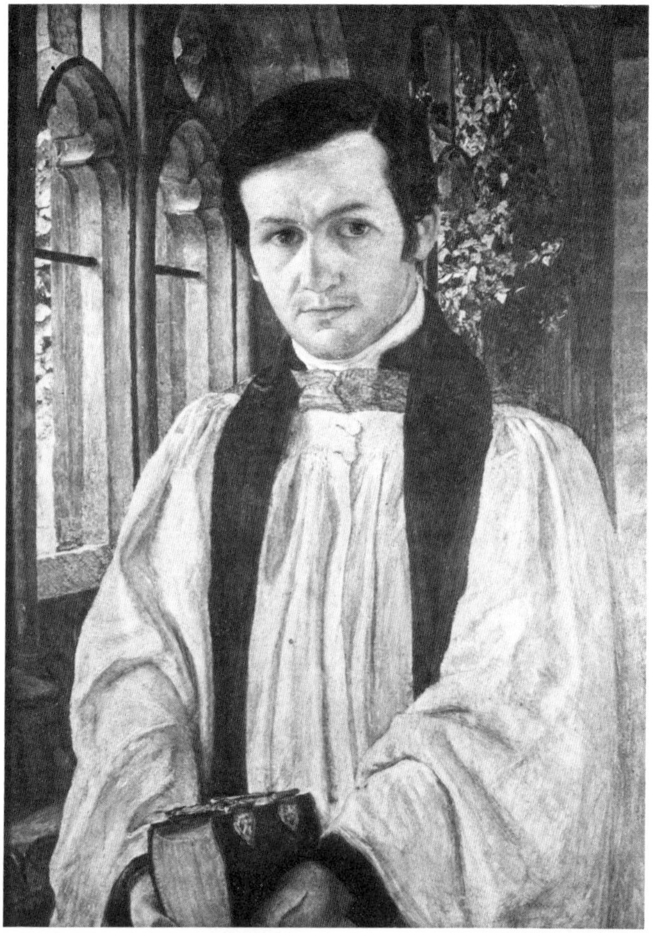

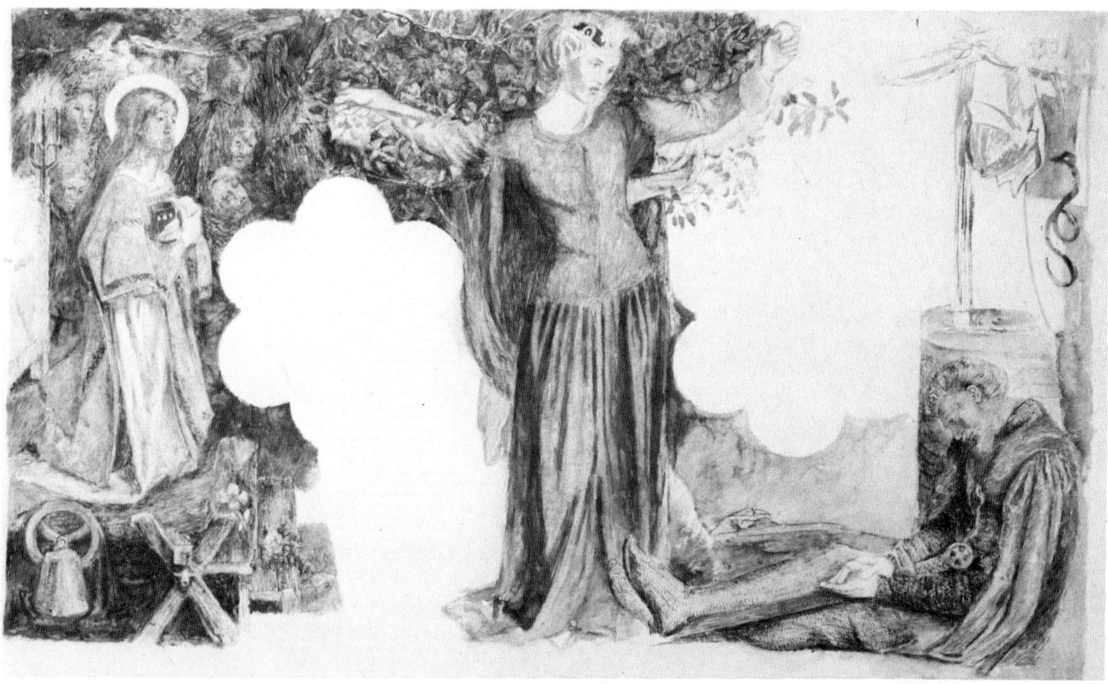

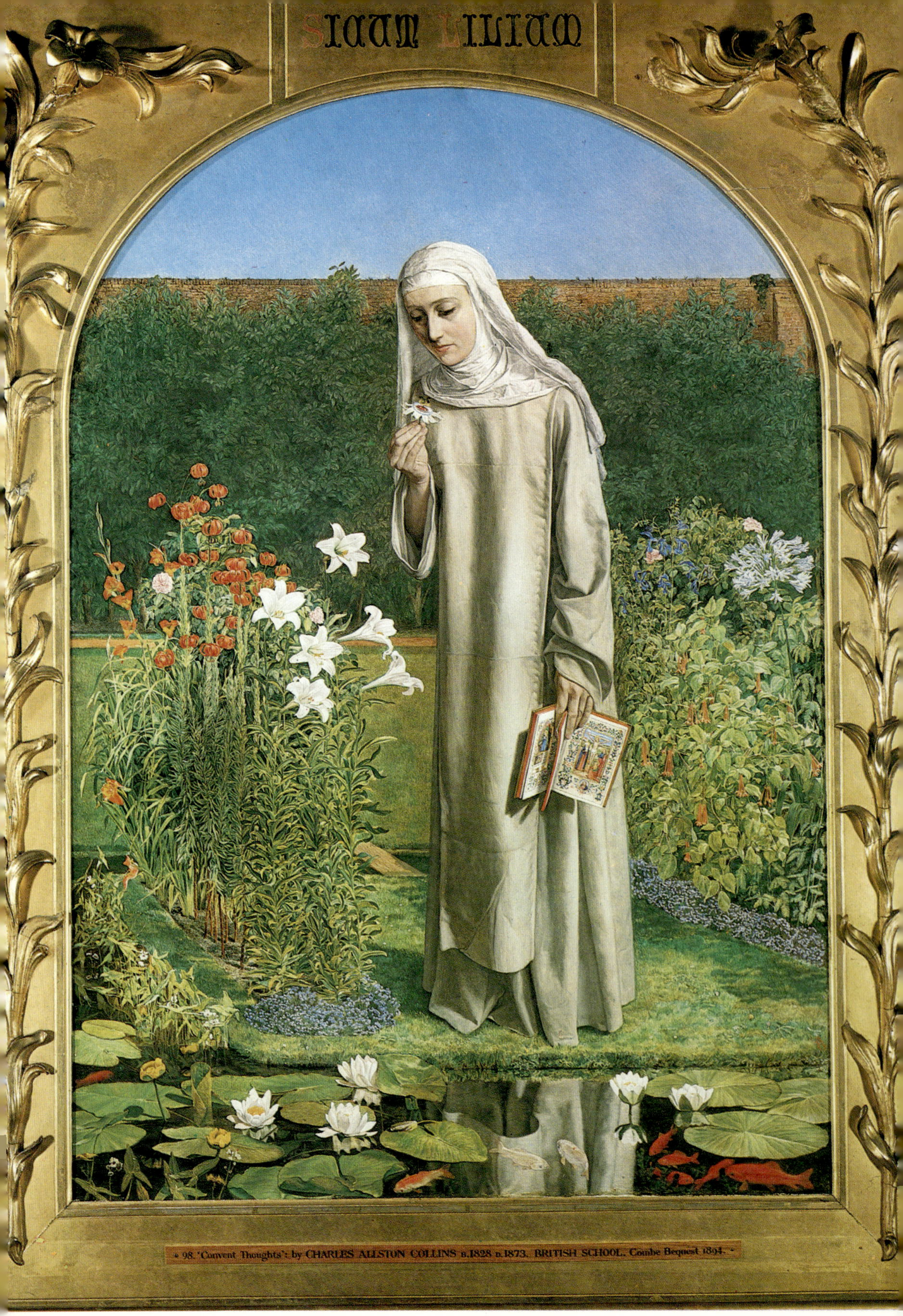
SICUT LILIUM
• 98. 'Convent Thoughts': by CHARLES ALLSTON COLLINS B.1828 D.1873. BRITISH SCHOOL. Combe Bequest 1894. •

The main works Millais produced for Combe were *The Return of the Dove to the Ark* and a portrait of his benefactor with a cat in his lap; accompanying these in Combe's collection were Charles Collins's *Convent Thoughts*, painted in the patron's garden, and the picture by Hunt mentioned above (all now in the Ashmolean). But the most celebrated of his paintings was Hunt's *The Light of the World*, which he bought in 1854 for 400 guineas. Shortly after his death, Combe's widow presented *The Light of the World* to Keble College, where it now hangs, in a specially built side-chapel to the south of the chapel itself. Combe was a devout churchman – he was deeply involved in the Oxford Movement – and through him the Pre-Raphaelites became acquainted with a number of clergymen. One of these was the Reverend J. D. Jenkins, whose portrait Hunt painted in the setting of New College Cloisters.

In its nostalgia for medieval Christianity the Oxford Movement had a clear tie of sympathy with Pre-Raphaelitism, the very name of which signified a reverence for art and life before the Renaissance. This tie is exemplified in Thomas Combe, and also in the careers of the 'second generation' Pre-Raphaelites William Morris and Edward Burne-Jones. The two men came up to Exeter College together in 1853, became friends, and eventually occupied adjoining rooms (these were demolished during the rebuilding of the college in the later 1850s). They both intended to take Orders and were already fired with enthusiasm for the Oxford Movement and anything connected with the Middle Ages. They avidly read Chaucer and Malory, they studied illuminated manuscripts in the Bodleian Library, and would make pilgrimages to the ruined nunnery at Godstowe, the supposed burial-place of the Fair Rosamund. 'I came back in a delirium of joy, the land was so enchanted with bright colours, blue purple in the sky, shot over with a shower of golden dust,' wrote Burne-Jones after one visit to the place, 'and in my mind pictures of the old days, the abbey, and long processions of the faithful, banners of the cross, copes and crosiers, gay knights and ladies by the river bank.'

In 1854 Morris and Burne-Jones saw their first Pre-Raphaelite painting, Millais's *The Return of the Dove to the Ark*, which was on display at Wyatt's shop in the High Street. Amazed and excited, they went to see the rest of Combe's collection and were introduced to the work of the Pre-Raphaelite who was most to influence them, Dante Gabriel Rossetti. They met Rossetti in Oxford during the following year and his charismatic personality reinforced their admiration. Theology now came to take second place to art and both men abandoned the idea of joining the clergy. After a tour of French cathedrals during the long vacation of their second year, they decided to leave Oxford for London, Morris to train as an architect and Burne-Jones as a painter, under Rossetti's supervision.

Rossetti visited Oxford again in 1857, and during his stay went to see the new Debating Hall (now the Library) of the Oxford Union. (It is a curious coincidence that the Union's previous meeting-place had been a hall belonging to James Wyatt, behind his High Street premises.) The spaces above the bookshelves in the gallery seemed to Rossetti to call out for painted decorations; he promptly proposed himself for the job and both the architect and the Union welcomed the idea. The murals would show incidents from the *Morte d'Arthur* and would be executed free of charge by Rossetti and a team of assistants: Burne-Jones and Morris, whom he had persuaded to give up architecture for painting, Arthur Hughes, Val Prinsep, Spencer Stanhope and John Hungerford Pollen.

The work was carried out in an atmosphere of hilarity and high jinks, encouraged by no inconsiderable amount of alcohol. The young Swinburne, who was then an undergraduate at Balliol and had become friendly with the artists, recalled a characteristic incident involving 'two respectable members of the University' who came to see the decorations in progress: 'We spoke just then of kisses in Paradise, and expounded our ideas on the celestial development of that necessity of life; and after listening for five minutes to our language, they literally fled from the room! Conceive our mutual ecstasy of delight.' The murals were painted in an amateurish technique and began to fade almost as soon as they were finished; attempts to restore them have not been successful and today they are virtually invisible. While working on them, Morris, Burne-Jones and Rossetti all lived together at 87 High Street (now a bank) and later at 13 George Street (gone).

John Ruskin, the critic and champion of Pre-Raphaelitism, was also closely associated with Oxford. He was an undergraduate at Christ Church from 1837 to 1839, living successively on the north side of Peckwater Quadrangle, in Tom Quad (staircase 4, first floor left), and in lodgings

OPPOSITE: Charles Allston Collins *Convent Thoughts* 1850–1; oil on canvas, 84 × 59 cm Ashmolean Museum, Oxford

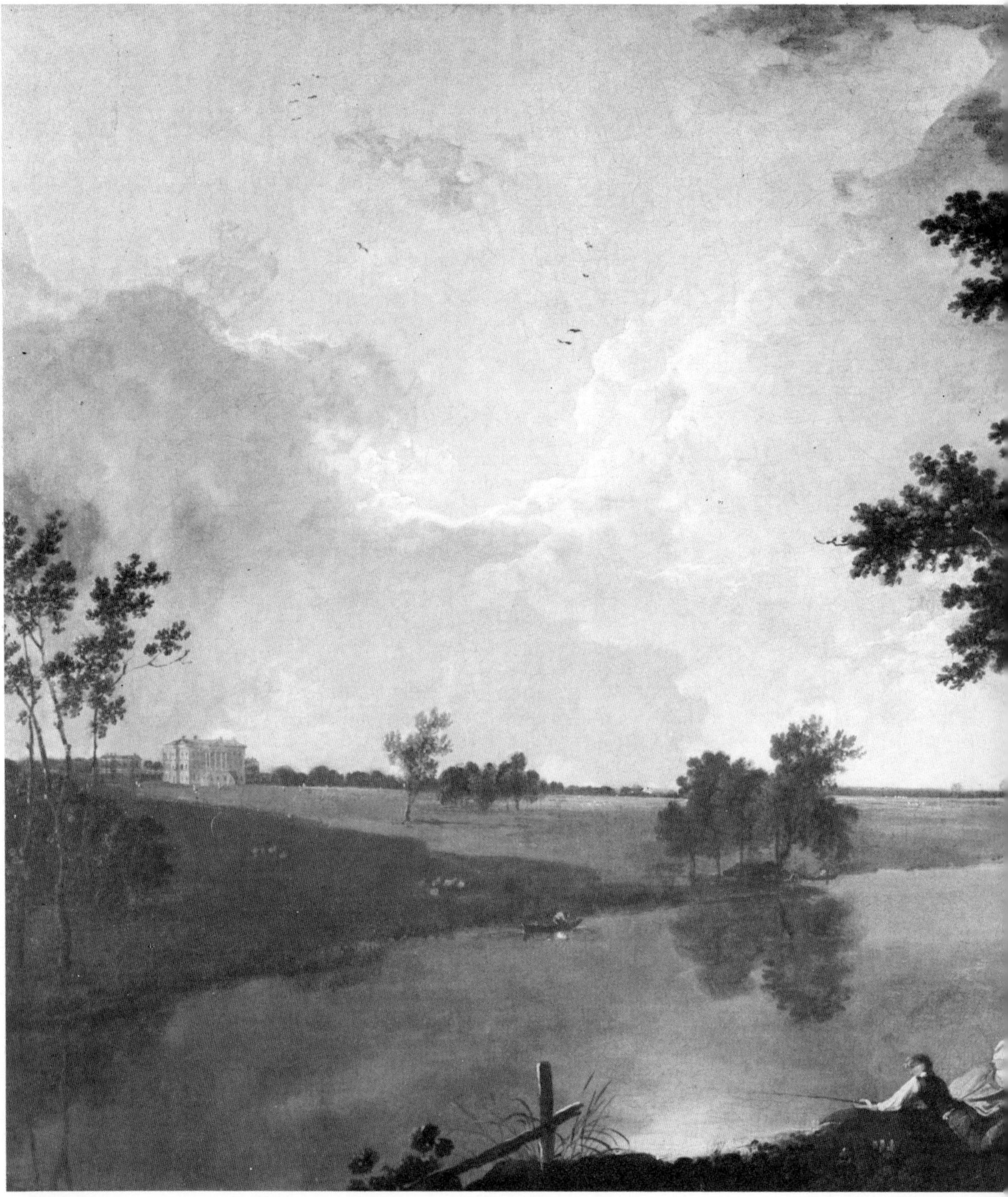

Richard Wilson
Tabley House
c. 1774; oil on canvas, 100·3 × 125·8 cm
Private collection

in St Aldate's, although he spent much of his time with his mother, who came up during terms and lived at 90 High Street. Ruskin's involvement with the building of the University Museum entailed being in Oxford frequently in the 1850s, and it was he who first brought Rossetti here, by suggesting that the artist's companion Elizabeth Siddal should take medical advice from his friend Dr Acland. In 1870 Ruskin became the first Slade Professor of Fine Art in the University, a post he held for fifteen years. Soon after the appointment he established his Drawing School in the Ashmolean, endowing it with a large number of drawings, prints and photographs from his own collection. But his most famous act as Professor was to set a

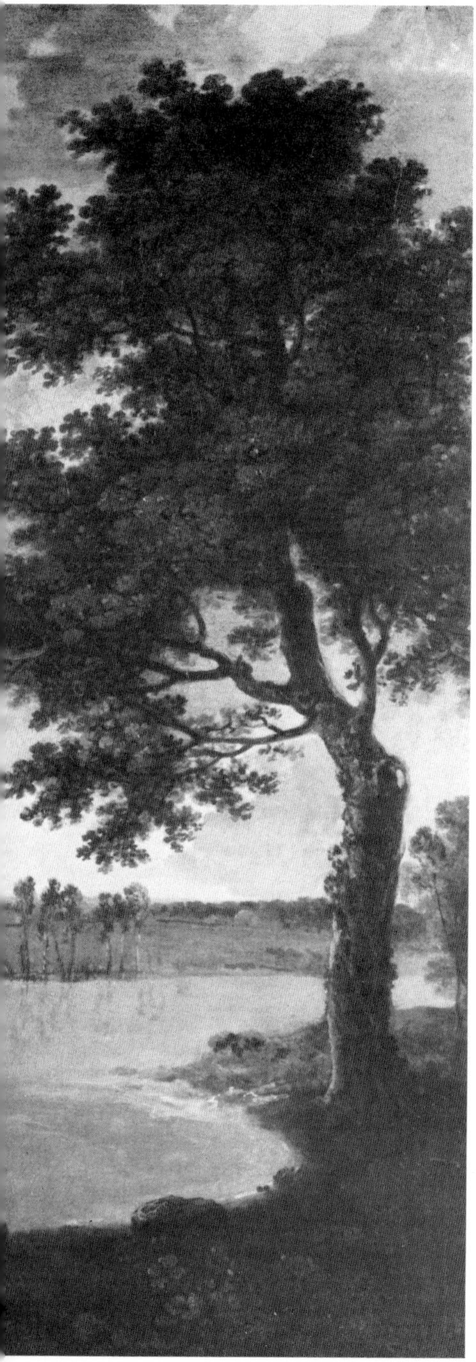

group of undergraduates, including Oscar Wilde, to repair a stretch of road between Oxford and Ferry Hinksey so that they might 'feel the pleasures of useful muscular work'. During his Professorship Ruskin lived in the Fellows' Building (staircase 2, first floor right) in Corpus Christi, and would occasionally go out to Abingdon and stay at the Crown and Thistle.

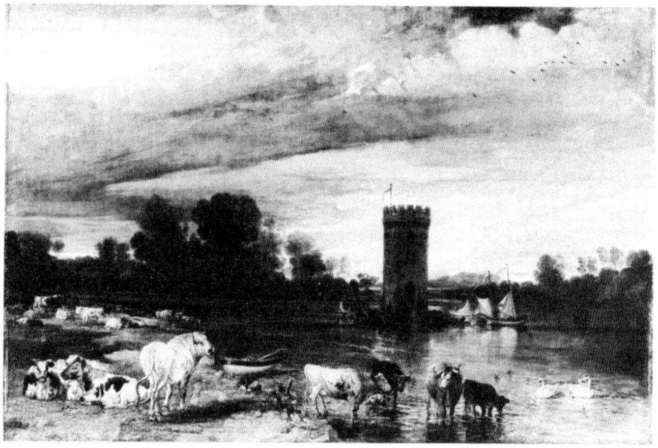

James Ward
Lake and Tower in Tabley Park
1814; oil on canvas, 94 × 136 cm
Tate Gallery, London

Painswick, *Glos.*

The most distinguished painters of the Cotswolds were William Rothenstein, who lived at Far Oakridge (q.v.), and Charles Gere. Gere was born in Gloucester, and attended the Birmingham School of Art in the 1880s. Birmingham at that time was a centre both of the Arts and Crafts Movement and the Tempera Revival. While at the School, Gere attracted the attention of William Morris, who commissioned him to produce illustrations for the Kelmscott Press. Gere and his painter sister Margaret came to Painswick in 1904 and stayed here for most of their lives. The landscapes of Gere are generally small and painted in tempera; in the lyrical simplicity of his works he follows in the poetic tradition of Samuel Palmer and Edward Calvert.

Quarrington, *Lincs.*

The rectory in Quarrington was the birthplace of the painter Charles Shannon, who was born in 1863. He grew up here but spent most of his life in London, living with the designer Charles Ricketts. Shannon's homosexuality and high aestheticism caused his family at home a great deal of embarrassment. He died in 1937 and is buried in Quarrington churchyard.

Seagrave, *Leics.*

Seagrave, about eight miles north-east of Leicester, was the home village of the sporting painter Ben Marshall. Born here in 1768, he worked locally as a schoolmaster until moving to London at the age of twenty-three to train as an artist. Marshall spent most of his career in London and Newmarket, but many of his works were commissioned by Leicestershire huntsmen.

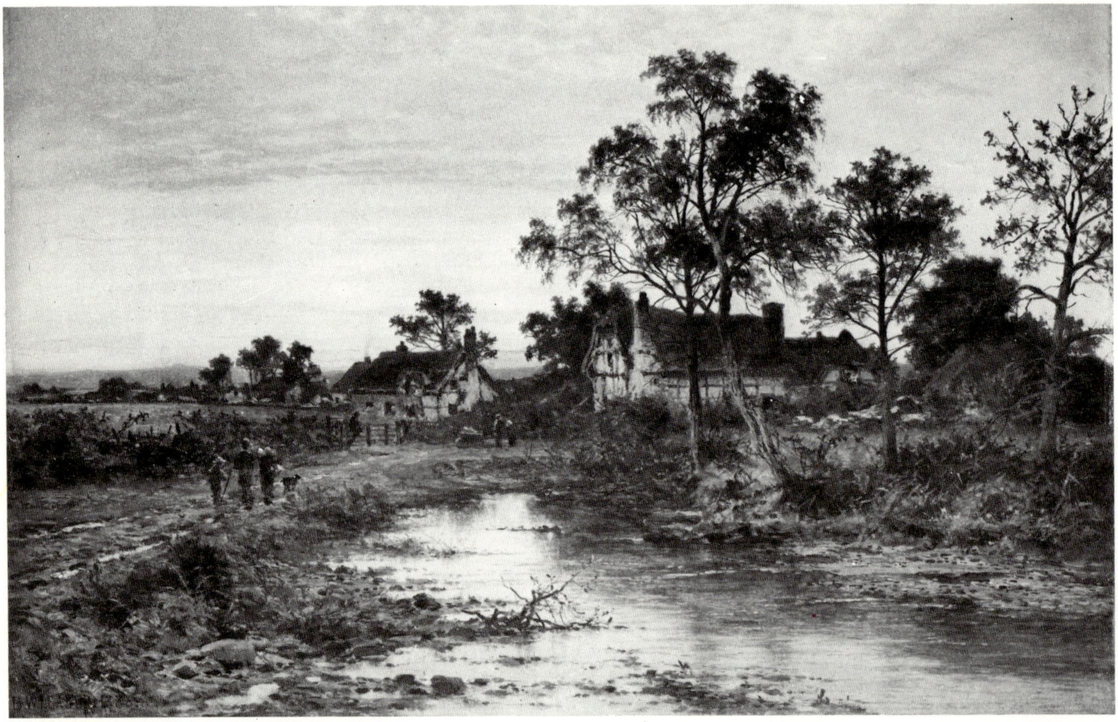

Benjamin Williams Leader
Worcester Landscape
1886; oil on canvas,
61·2×91·6 cm
Walker Art Gallery,
Liverpool

Tabley, *Cheshire*

Just off the A556 near Knutsford, Tabley was until recently the seat of the Leicester family, who were important patrons of British art in the eighteenth and early nineteenth centuries. Sir Peter Leicester commissioned portraits of himself from Arthur Devis and of the estate from Richard Wilson. His son, Sir John, had views of Tabley painted by Turner and James Ward, both of them featuring the lake and the tower, a castellated Gothic folly surrounded by water. Ward was understandably apprehensive about following in the footsteps of Wilson and Turner. 'I have had to tell a story that has been told before so beautifully as to make me tremble,' he wrote. 'By a more rigid attention to truth', however, he felt he had succeeded in producing something original. Tabley, which still contains much of the Leicester collection, is now the property of the University of Manchester. It is not open to the public but interested visitors are shown round by the agents for the estate.

Whitchurch, *Hereford and Worcester*

Whitchurch was the childhood home of Philip Wilson Steer. His family came to Herefordshire from Birkenhead in 1864, and moved to The Grange on the village's main street. Steer's father later renamed their home Apsley House in honour of the Duke of Wellington. The father – who died when Steer was only eleven – arranged a museum for the children in Apsley House and encouraged them to become ardent collectors of shells, plants and minerals; this interest was retained by the artist in later life. Around 1878 he went to study at the Gloucester School of Art, but still continued to live at home. The journey was so long that he was only able to attend three times a week. Eventually he was advised to live nearer the School, and in consequence his mother sold Apsley House and took a home in Gloucester itself. As a mature artist Steer spent much of his time painting in the Welsh Marches, and did a whole series of landscapes around Ludlow, Bridgnorth and Chepstow.

Worcester, *Hereford and Worcester*

The father of the landscape painter Benjamin Williams Leader was a distinguished civil engineer who worked for the Severn Navigation Commission. The family lived at Diglis House (now the Diglis Hotel), near the cathedral and overlooking the river, and it was here that the artist was born in 1831. Leader's work includes many views of Worcester and the surrounding countryside.